Disclaimer: The opinions presented herein are solely those of the author except where specifically noted. Nothing in the book should be construed as investment advice or guidance, as it is not intended as investment advice or guidance, nor is it offered as such. Nothing in the book should be construed as a recommendation to buy or sell any financial or physical asset. It is solely the opinion of the writer, who is not an investment professional. The publisher/author disclaims any implied warranty or applicability of the contents for any particular purpose. The publisher/author shall not be liable for any commercial or incidental damages of any kind or nature.

First edition published September 2022

Oftwominds.com
P.O. Box 10847
Hilo HI 96721

Cover: Theresa Barzyk

Self-Reliance in the 21st Century

Charles Hugh Smith

With gratitude to everyone who has taught someone a skill that advances self-reliance.

Table of Contents

Chapter One: Self-Reliance Then and Now

The Difference Between Self-Reliance in 1841 and the 21st Century

What is self-reliance?

Ralph Waldo Emerson's advice in his 1841 essay *Self-Reliance* still rings true today: "*Be yourself; no base imitator of another, but your best self. There is something which you can do better than another.*"

For Emerson, self-reliance means thinking independently, trusting your own intuition and refusing to take the well-worn path of conforming to others' expectations.

This celebration of individualism is the norm today, but it was radical in Emerson's more traditionalist day. What's striking about Emerson's description of self-reliance is its internal quality: it's about one's intellectual and emotional self-reliance, not the hands-on skills of producing life's essentials.

Emerson doesn't describe self-reliance in terms of taking care of oneself in practical terms, such as being able to build a cabin on Walden Pond and live off foraging and a garden like his friend Thoreau. (The land on Walden Pond was owned by Emerson.)

Emerson did not address practical self-reliance because these skills were commonplace in the largely agrarian, rural 1840s. Even city dwellers mostly made their living from practical skills, and the majority of their food came from nearby farms. (Imported sugar, coffee, tea and spices were luxuries.)

The economy of the 1840s was what we would now call *localized*: most of the goods and services were locally produced, and households provided many of their own basic needs. Global trade in commodities such as tea and porcelain thrived, but these luxuries made up a small part of the economy (one exception being whale oil used for lighting).

Even in the 1840s, few individuals were as self-sufficient as Thoreau. Households met many of their needs themselves, but they relied on *trusted personal networks* of makers and suppliers for whatever goods and services they could not provide themselves.

Households sold their surplus production of homemade goods and family businesses offered small-scale production of specialty goods (metal forging, furniture, etc.) and services (printing, legal documents, etc.).

For example, Thoreau's family business was manufacturing pencils and supplying graphite (pencil lead). Before he took over this business on the death of his father, he earned his living as a surveyor.

Households obtained what they needed from local networks of suppliers who were known to them. If some item was needed from afar, the local source had their own network of trusted suppliers.

The government's role was also limited. The government provided postal, judicial and basic education systems and collected tariffs on trade, but its role in everyday life beyond these essential services was modest.

The conditions of Emerson and Thoreau's day—localized hands-on self-reliance was the norm and the elevation of the individual was radical—have reversed: now the celebration of the individual is the norm while few have practical skills. Our economy is *globalized*, with few if any of the goods and services we rely on being sourced locally. We rely on government and corporations for the essentials of life. Few of us know anyone who actually produces essentials.

Our primary means of obtaining the staples of life is shopping because producing basics ourselves is difficult compared to getting everything we need from global supply chains.

Emerson took the practical skills of self-reliance for granted because these skills were the bedrock of everyday life. Now skills have become specialized: we gain narrow expertise to earn our living and only hobbyists develop multiple skills.

What is self-reliance in the 21st century?

Some may feel that having a job--being *self-supporting*--is self-reliance, but relying solely on goods and services from afar isn't self-reliance. Should a few links in those long supply chains break, the entire chain collapses and we're helpless.

Money only has value when it's scarce. When money is abundant and essentials of life are scarce, money loses value. When supply chains break down, money is a measure of our helplessness, not our self-reliance.

The inner self-reliance Emerson described as *being our best selves* remains essential, but the material-world skills of self-reliance have atrophied. We rely on government and long supply chains for our necessities without understanding the fragility of these complex systems.

In the 21st century, even more than in the 1840s, self-reliance doesn't mean *self-sufficiency*. Even Thoreau used nails and tools produced elsewhere. Building a cabin on a remote pond isn't practical for most of us, and even Thoreau re-entered conventional life after two years.

What self-reliance means in the 21st century is *reducing our dependence on complex systems we have no control over*. This means *reducing the number of links in our personal supply chains* and *reducing our dependence on goods and services from afar* by 1) *consuming less* and eliminating waste and planned obsolescence; 2) *learning how to do more for ourselves and others* so we need less from the government and global supply chains; 3) *relocalizing our personal supply chains* by assembling *trusted personal networks* of local producers and 4) *becoming a producer* in addition to being a consumer.

Just as Emerson noted that self-reliance requires being our best self--something no one else can do--no one else can chart our course to self-reliance. Our path must be our own, tailored to our unique circumstances.

Self-reliance in the 21st century means moving from the artifice of trying to appear grander than our real selves in social media to the authenticity of being a producer anchored by a self-reliance that no longer needs the approval of others.

Here are some examples of what I mean by self-reliance in the 21st century.

By becoming healthy, we need fewer (ideally zero) medications that are sourced from afar and we're less dependent on costly medical interventions.

By becoming a producer in a local network, we reduce the number of links in our supply chain from many to a few. If we trade for food from local producers, there are only a few links in that supply chain. If we grow some of our own food, there are zero links in that supply chain.

By eliminating waste, we reduce our dependency on distant sources of food, energy and water—what I call the FEW essentials. If we eliminate 40% of our consumption, we've reduced our dependency on supply chains we don't control by 40%.

By buying durable products that we can repair ourselves, we reduce our dependency on the global system of planned obsolescence and waste that I call the *Landfill Economy*. The less we need and the less we waste, the lower our dependency on fragile supply chains and the greater our self-reliance.

By moving to a location near fresh water, food and energy, we reduce our exposure to the risks of long supply chains breaking down.

The more we provide for ourselves, the less we need from unsustainable systems we don't control.

Self-reliance has many other benefits. Self-reliance gives us purpose, meaning, goals, fulfillment, enjoyment and the means to help others.

Specialization and Fragility

Our economy is *optimized* (i.e., streamlined) for specialization because that's how our economy became more productive. By mastering one skill, each worker can produce more than non-specialists. This is one of the key insights of Adam Smith's *Wealth of Nations*, published in 1776: the *comparative advantages* of specialization increase the wealth of both buyer and seller.

As the global economy has become more cost-sensitive, specialization has increased. Enterprises want highly productive workers and this requires specialization.

The higher our skill, the more valuable we are and the more we earn. The financial incentives favor specialization rather than broadening our real-world skills.

The financial incentives for developing real-world self-reliance are marginal. If repairing a toaster takes two hours and we're paid $25 an hour at our job, that's $50 of time. If a new toaster costs $25, why bother learning how to repair the broken one? Hobbyists may repair things, but for most people, it makes sense to devote their time to making money and toss the broken toaster in the landfill.

This is why we have a *Landfill Economy*. We measure prosperity by how much gets tossed in the landfill and replaced with something new. If we measured prosperity by how long products last and how easy they are to repair, we'd have much different incentives and a much different economy.

Valuing everything in terms of time and convenience makes sense in an era of endless abundance but it breaks down in an era of scarcity. If things are no longer cheap and accessible with an on-screen click, then the calculation of what's valuable changes.

The conveniences of the 21st century come at a cost few recognize: our dependence on long supply chains that are inherently fragile. These chains of specialized production and distribution we depend on only function if every link works perfectly, but things are no longer working perfectly. These long supply chains are decaying right before our eyes.

The era of abundance has ended and we're not prepared for an era of scarcity.

Since few of us know anyone who produces anything tangible, our social networks are completely disconnected from the production of life's essentials. We're completely dependent on products made thousands of miles away delivered by supply chains powered by diesel.

As these systems decay and scarcities drive prices higher, the incentives change. What becomes convenient and low-cost is producing essentials within our own local networks. Specialization will still be valuable in terms of producing surplus which can be traded or sold locally, but specialization is no substitute for practical knowledge.

Abundance gave us the time and means to express our uniqueness on social media. In a world of scarcity, our uniqueness will find expression in becoming productive in a network of other producers.

Self-reliance in the 21st century demands both the inner strengths Emerson promoted and the real-world skills and trusted local networks he took for granted that we have lost.

Many people believe that scarcities are temporary and abundance will soon be restored. They are mistaken, and it's important to understand why.

What Are the Essentials of Human Life?

Before we address scarcity, we need to define *essentials*. There are two ways of thinking about the essentials of human life: one is psychologist Abraham Maslow's *hierarchy of needs*, which many visualize as a pyramid of physiological needs as the base, with the higher levels being security and love, belonging and self-worth, and what Emerson called *being our best selves*, what we now call *self-actualization*.

In this approach, food, water, clothing, shelter and energy are the basic physiological needs without which we perish. Above basic survival, we need safety / security and belonging to a supportive family and group. Above those basic emotional needs, we need self-respect. At the top of the pyramid is becoming our best selves via self-knowledge and self-expression.

The second approach is to look at the complex system that provides our basic needs as an iceberg where 90% of the system is not discernable. For example, we think of food being available at supermarkets without grasping the immense system that grows and harvests the grains, raises and slaughters the animals, processes and packages all these products and delivers them thousands of miles to markets near us. The systems that provide us with fresh water, clothing, shelter and fuel are equally complex and costly.

In other words, our food supply doesn't just rely on farms and farmers. It relies on roads and diesel fuel, because the vast majority of our food travels hundreds of miles on trucks. It depends on spare parts being available for tractors, trucks, aircraft and many other machines such as freezers, as well as parts for the oil wells, pipelines and refineries that provide diesel fuel for the tractors and trucks.

The grapes flown in from thousands of miles away require jet fuel, air cargo containers, refrigerants and spare parts for jet engines.

Many of our basic essentials come from overseas: fabric and clothing, minerals such as cobalt and the materials needed to make pharmaceuticals.

These long supply chains need millions of machines to work perfectly to function. All these machines depend on a vast industrial base for their manufacture, maintenance and operation.

Compare these fantastically complex and costly 21st century systems without which the basics of human life disappear with the sources of essentials in Emerson's 19th century America. Food was grown within walking distance even for city-folk, clothing was often sewn at home and shelter was built out of local materials.

If we look at these systems as networks with nodes and connections, we ask: how many intermediary links are there between the source of the food and our table? In the 19th century, there was often no intermediary link at all: the harvest was turned into food within walking distance. Now there are dozens of links in every chain connecting us to the sources of what we need to survive.

If even one link in those chains fails, the chain is broken.

What are the essentials of human life nowadays? Food, water, clothing, shelter and energy, and all the parts of the vast industrial system that processes and delivers these essentials to us.

The greater our dependence on long, complex chains, the lower our self-reliance because we cannot possibly influence these chains. If they break, we're helpless. Our only leverage is to reduce our dependency on these chains and reduce the number of intermediary links between the source of essentials and our household.

Reducing dependencies and shortening our supply chains are the core principles of self-reliance in the 21st century.

We cannot reduce our dependency on complex, costly supply chains to zero, but we can reduce our dependency in consequential ways. Which is preferable: to be 100% dependent on long supply chains for food, or source half of your food within walking distance? Which is preferable: to need 100 gallons of fuel a month just to get by, or 10 gallons?

Let's look at why self-reliance will become increasingly valuable as unsustainable systems start breaking down.

Global Disruptions Are Affecting Everything and Everyone

The conventional media has a vested interest in maintaining confidence in the status quo, and so blunt realities are softened into acceptable pablum. For example, globalization is presented as win-win for everyone, when the blunt reality is the benefits flowed to the few at the expense of the many: American corporate profits soared from less than $700 billion in 2002 just after China entered the World Trade Organization (WTO) to $3.4 trillion annually in 2022.

While America's economy (GDP) rose 2.3-fold in those 20 years, corporate profits soared almost five-fold. (Source: St. Louis Federal Reserve Bank.)

This astounding increase in corporate profits was not a happy accident.

Corporate profits soared because Corporate America (along with other global corporations) shipped production to China and other low-wage, lax environmental standards nations, cutting costs and quality while keeping prices high. Pressured by globalization, the wages of American workers lost ground.

Globalization was never win-win; it was win-lose: those reaping the immense profits won and everyone else lost. Yes, the cost of a few products dropped, but the quality dropped even more. Corners were cut to boost profits and so the poor-quality product soon ended up in the landfill. Before globalization, products lasted decades; after globalization, they only last a few years and have to be replaced. How is that a win for consumers?

Now the boom in China is unraveling, and once again we're not being told the blunt reality: corporations are shifting production out of

China because the changing political and economic landscape is threatening their fat profits.

The dynamics disrupting the global economy are presented piecemeal, when in fact each source of disruption reinforces the others.

Once we understand the self-reinforcing nature of these disruptions, we realize the global system is changing permanently and these changes will affect everyone. These disruptions are not temporary or trivial. They are long-term and cannot be reversed, any more than time can be reversed.

1. Climate change. Drought, flooding and extreme temperatures are disrupting agriculture and pushing habitable regions into being uninhabitable. Food will be scarce and expensive. (See the following section on the end of cheap food.)

2. Disease and pandemics. Global air travel enables mutations and rapid spread of microbes.

3. Long supply chains. (See following sections.) These fragile chains are disrupted by pandemics, geopolitical conflicts, economic and labor turmoil and scarcities of essential commodities.

4. Domestic political turmoil. Global sources of disruption--soaring energy and food prices, hardship caused by climate change, financial bubbles popping--fuel political discontent.

5. Labor discontent. Demographics and labor shortages are pushing global wages higher; workers are demanding living wages, leading to strikes and other disruptions.

6. Depletion of cheap, easy-to-get resources. If energy is still abundant, why are we drilling so deep in such inhospitable places and mining tar sands? The low hanging fruit has been picked, what's left is hard to get. This can't be reversed.

7. War and conflict. Wars to control resources are disrupting supply chains and globalization. Wars are being waged on numerous fronts: cyber warfare, proxy warfare, Cold Wars, hot wars, rebellions, etc.

8. Unraveling of global finance. Currencies, credit, risk and assets are all being repriced. Volatility is now the norm.

Everyone who is dependent on the global economy for goods, services and income has become dependent on a system that is unraveling. Disruptions in one region quickly spread, eventually affecting everyone. One domino topples a line of other dominoes that end up knocking down all the dominoes.

The idea that all these sources of disruption will go away and all the dominoes of global abundance can be set up again is not realistic. What's realistic is to start reducing our dependence on long supply chains by relocalizing our production of life's essentials. Since we can't count on authorities being willing or able to move fast enough to matter, the best option is to relocalize our own supply chains and reduce our dependence on systems that are unraveling. The term that describes this is *self-reliance*.

Our Unsustainable Economy in a Nutshell: Energy and Resources

Beneath its surface stability, our economy is precarious because the foundation of the global economy-- cheap energy--has reached an inflection point: from now on, energy will become more expensive. There will be temporary drops in price but over time, the trend is higher costs and more frequent shortages.

The problem is the price can't be high enough for producers to earn enough to reinvest in more production and low enough for consumers to afford it. Consumers will not have enough money left after paying for energy to spend freely on discretionary goods and services, so the consumer economy will shrink.

For the hundred years that resources were cheap and abundant, we could waste everything and call it growth: when an appliance went to the landfill because it was designed to fail (planned obsolescence) so a new one would have to be purchased. That waste was called *growth* because the Gross Domestic Product (GDP) went up when the replacement was purchased.

A million vehicles idling in a traffic jam is also called *growth* because more gasoline was consumed, even though the gasoline was wasted.

This is why the global economy is a *waste is growth Landfill Economy*. The faster something ends up in the landfill, the higher the growth.

Now that we've consumed all the easy-to-get resources, all that's left is costly to extract. For example, minerals buried in mountains hundreds of miles from paved roads and harbors require enormous investments in infrastructure just to reach the deposits and ship them to distant mills and refineries. Oil deposits that are deep beneath the ocean floor are not cheap to get, regardless of what technology is used.

Does it really make sense to expect that the human population can triple and our consumption of energy increase ten-fold and there will always be enough resources to keep supplies abundant and prices low? No, it doesn't.

Many people believe that nuclear power (fusion, thorium reactors, mini-reactors, etc.) will provide cheap, safe electricity that will replace hydrocarbons (oil and natural gas). But nuclear power is inherently costly, and the technologies many pin their hopes on are still being developed. They are years or even decades away from generating electricity for consumers.

Reactors take many years to construct and are costly to build and maintain. Cost over-runs are common. A new reactor in Finland, for example, is nine years behind schedule and costs have tripled.

The U.S. has built only two new reactors in the past 25 years.

The world's 440 reactors supply about 10% of global electricity. There are currently 55 new reactors under construction in 19 countries, but it will take many years before they produce electricity. We would have to build a new reactor a week for many years to replace hydrocarbon-generated electricity. This scale of construction simply isn't practical.

Supplying all energy consumption globally--for all transportation, heating of buildings, etc.-- would require over 10,000 reactors by some estimates--over 20 times the current number of reactors in service.

Many believe so-called renewable energy such as solar and wind will replace hydrocarbons. But as analyst Nate Hagens has explained, these sources are not truly renewable, they are *replaceable*; all solar panels and wind turbines must be replaced at great expense every 20 to 25 years. These sources generate less than 5% of global energy, and it will take many decades of expansion to replace even half of the hydrocarbon fuels we currently consume.

To double the energy generated by wind/solar in 25 years, we'll need to build three for each one in service today: one to replace the existing one and two more to double the energy being produced.

Since wind and solar are intermittent sources of energy, we must maintain a backup system for when the sun goes down and the wind diminishes. This means the full cost of relying on intermittent sources is far higher than when we only had one system powered by hydrocarbon fuels: now we must pay to operate two systems rather than one.

All these intermittent sources require vast amounts of resources: diesel fuel for transport, materials for fabricating turbines, solar panels, concrete foundations, and so on.

Humans are wired to believe that whatever we have now will still be ours in the future. We don't like being told we'll have less of anything in the future.

The current solution is to create more money out of thin air in the belief that if we create more money, then more oil, copper, etc. will be found and extracted.

But this isn't really a solution. What happens if we add a zero to all our currency? If we add a zero to a $10 bill so it becomes $100, do we suddenly get ten times more food, gasoline, etc. with the new bill? No.

Prices quickly rise ten-fold so the new $100 bill buys the same amount as the old $10.

Adding zeroes to our money (*hyper-financialization*) doesn't make everything that's scarce and hard to get suddenly cheap and easy to get. Minerals are still scarce and hard to get no matter how many zeroes we add to our money.

Many people feel good about recycling a small part of what we consume. But recycling is not cost-free, and the majority of what we consume is not recycled.

The percentage of lithium batteries that are recycled, for example, is very low, less than 5%. We have to mine vast quantities of lithium because we dump 95% of all lithium batteries in the landfill. There are many reasons for this, one being that the batteries aren't designed to be recycled because this would cost more.

The majority of all manufactured goods--products that required immense amounts of hydrocarbons to make--are tossed in the landfill.

Our economy is precarious because it's in a lose-lose dilemma: resource prices can't stay high enough for producers to make a profit and reinvest without impoverishing consumers. Prices can't stay low enough to allow consumers to spend freely without producers losing money. If producers don't make enough to reinvest, supplies decline and scarcities increase.

Playing hyper-financialized games--creating money out of thin air, borrowing from tomorrow to spend more today and inflating speculative bubbles in stocks and housing--doesn't actually create more of what's scarce. All these financial games make wealth inequality worse (*hyper-inequality*), undermining social stability.

The economy has reached an inflection point where everything that is unsustainable finally starts unraveling. Each of these systems is dependent on all the other systems (what we call a *tightly bound system*), so when one critical system unravels, the crisis quickly spreads to the entire system: one domino falling knocks down all the dominoes snaking through the global economy.

Those who understand how tightly interconnected, unsustainable systems are effectively *designed to fail* can prepare themselves by becoming flexible and open to the opportunities that will arise as the economy shifts from the Landfill Economy's consumer spending to maintaining essential infrastructure.

The End of Cheap Food

Of all the modern-day miracles, perhaps the least appreciated is the incredible abundance of low-cost food in the U.S. and other developed countries.

The era of cheap food is ending, for a variety of interconnected reasons.

I have long had an interest in growing food, dating back to my teens 50 years ago. I have been a gardener for decades, but my knowledge has expanded over the past four years as we have sought to grow as much high-quality food as possible on our residential lot.

I've learned about food production from research, my *Of Two Minds* blog correspondents and my own experience of *hands in the dirt*.

What I've learned is that *every little bit helps*--even small backyards / rooftops / greenhouses can provide significant amounts of food and satisfaction.

I've also learned that almost every temperate *terroir*/micro-climate is suitable for some plants, herbs, trees and animals. (*Terroir* includes everything about a specific place: the sun exposure, soil type, climate variations, etc.)

Choosing crops that fit the terroir—i.e., they grow without much intervention—and nurturing a diversity of crops are key features of localized production

We've forgotten that big cities once raised much of the food consumed by residents. Small plots of land, rooftop gardens, backyard chicken coops, etc. can add up when they are encouraged rather than discouraged.

What's striking is how disconnected many of us are from the production of the food we take for granted.

A great many of us know virtually nothing about how food is grown, raised, harvested / slaughtered, processed and packaged.

Highly educated people cannot recognize a green bean plant because they've never seen one. They know nothing about soil or industrial farming. They've never cared for any of the animals that humans have tended for their milk, eggs and flesh for millennia.

Most of us take the industrial scale of agriculture and the resulting abundance for granted, as if it was a birthright rather than a brief period of reckless consumption of resources that is ending.

Trying to make money by growing food on a small scale is difficult because we're competing with industrial agriculture powered by hydrocarbons and low-cost labor in distant lands.

That said, it is possible to develop niche products with local support by consumers and businesses. This is the *Half-X, Half-Farmer* model I've discussed in my blog: if the household has at least one part-time job that pays a decent wage, the household can pursue a less financially rewarding niche in agriculture/animal husbandry.

Industrial agriculture includes many elements few fully understand. The shipping of fruit thousands of miles via air freight is a function of 1)

cheap jet fuel and 2) global tourism, which fills airliners with passengers who subsidize the air cargo stored beneath their feet.

When global tourism dried up in the Covid lockdown, so did air cargo capacity.

I have to chuckle when I read an article about a new agricultural robot that will replace human labor, as if human labor were the key cost in industrial agriculture. Fertilizer, fuel, transport, animal feed, compliance costs, land leases and taxes are all major costs that robots don't eliminate. Furthermore, robots have their own operational and maintenance costs.

Left unsaid is the reliance of industrial agriculture on soil, fresh-water aquifers and rain. Irrigation is the result of rain/snow somewhere upstream. If it doesn't rain or snow upstream, the water needed for irrigation dries up.

Once the soil and aquifers are depleted and rain become erratic, the robot will be roaming a barren field.

The entirety of global food production rests on soil and rain. Robots don't change that.

What few of us who rely on industrial agriculture understand is that it depletes soil and drains aquifers by its very nature (i.e., maximize yield and profit today, never mind about tomorrow), and these resources cannot be replaced with technology. Once they're gone, they're gone.

Soil can be rebuilt but it can't be rebuilt by spreading fertilizers derived from natural gas over industrial-scale tracts of land.

Few people appreciate that the dirt is itself alive, and once it's dead it loses fertility. Whatever can be coaxed from depleted soil by chemical fertilizers lacks the micronutrients that plants, animals and humans all need.

Every organism is bound by the *Law of Minimums*: heaping on a few nutrients is useless unless all the other essential nutrients are available in the right quantities. For example, dumping excessive nitrogen fertilizer on a field won't make it yield more unless it has sufficient calcium, zinc, sulfur, magnesium, etc. All adding more nitrogen fertilizer does is poison waterways as the excess nitrogen runs off.

Irrigation is another part of industrial agriculture few understand. Over time, the natural salts in water build up in irrigated soil and the soil loses fertility. The drier the climate, the less rain there is to leach the salts from the soil. Irrigation isn't sustainable over the long run.

Plants need reliable conditions to reach maturity. Should a plant be starved of water and nutrients, its immune system weakens and it is more vulnerable to diseases and insects.

Extreme weather wreaks havoc on industrial agriculture. A crop can take months to reach maturity, and then a pounding rain can ruin the entire harvest in a few hours.

Most people assume there will always be an abundance of grains (rice, wheat, corn) without realizing that the vast majority of the world's grains come from a handful of regions with optimum conditions for industrial agriculture.

Should any of these places suffer erratic weather, then exports of grains will shrink dramatically. Once cheap grains are gone, cheap meat is also gone, because industrial-scale meat production depends on grain feed.

The scale required to grow an abundance of grain is monumental. Great expanses of Iowa, for example, are fields of corn and soybeans, much of which becomes animal feed.

American tourists who ooh and ahh over artisanal goat cheese in French or Italian villages have little appreciation for the human labor that goes into the artisanal food, labor that can't be replaced by robots except at industrial levels of production.

Industrial agriculture only works at vast *economies of scale* and *high utilization rates*. A 10-pound bag of chicken thighs is only $25 because tens of millions of chickens are raised in carefully engineered factory conditions and slaughtered / cleaned on an industrial scale.

Economies of scale lower costs by spreading the costs of labor and overhead—the factory equipment, maintenance, insurance, administration, etc.—over millions of units rather hundreds of units. If the factory produces a million units with the same workforce rather than a thousand units, the cost per unit will drop substantially.

To maintain the low cost per unit, the factory has to run at close to full capacity—the utilization rate has to be high. If production declines from one million units per month to 100,000 units a month for whatever reason—a shortage of materials, disruption of deliveries, a labor strike—the cost per unit rises sharply, and the company's profits drop.

Should the utilization rate fall over time, the operation ceases to be economically viable. No business can operate at a loss for long, and so production is shut down.

The global scale of industrial agriculture relies on exploiting low-cost labor forces and soil that hasn't yet been depleted. This is why clear-cutting the Amazon is so profitable: hire desperate workers with few other options to earn cash money, strip the soil until it's infertile and then move on.

It's slash-and-burn agriculture on an industrial scale.

There are many misunderstandings about industrial agriculture's reliance on cheap fuel and fertilizers derived from natural gas. Many pin their hopes on organic vegetables without realizing every organic tomato is still 5 teaspoons of diesel and 5 teaspoons of jet fuel if it's grown on an industrial scale and shipped via air. The organic vegetable is only less energy-intensive if it's grown locally on small-scale farms.

Much of the planet is not conducive to high-yield agriculture. The rain and weather are not suitable, or the soil is poor. Building up soil is a multi-year process of patient investment that isn't profitable for industrial agriculture.

Much of the grain we rely on is not easy to grow and process. It must be harvested, threshed, sorted, dried, milled, protected from insects and decay and then shipped thousands of miles. The price of rice, flour and corn meal is only low if the entire process is mechanized.

As a means to make money, small-scale food production can't compete with industrial agriculture. But that's not the goal of self-reliance.

The goal is to reduce our dependence on diesel-powered industrial agriculture by increasing our own local production, and grow a surplus that helps feed our trusted network of family, friends and neighbors.

As industrial agriculture depletes the last of its soils and aquifers, as fuels and fertilizers become increasingly costly, and as weather extremes disrupt the 50+ years of relatively reliable weather we've enjoyed, cheap food will vanish.

Once the scale and utilization rates decay, industrial agriculture will no longer be viable economically or environmentally.

In other words, industrial agriculture simply isn't sustainable. It's not a theory or a forecast, it's an observation. What most view as "impossible"—the end of cheap food-- is inevitable.

As industrial agriculture decays, food will become much more expensive. Even if it doubles in price, it will still be cheap compared to what it may cost in the future.

Few appreciate the potential productivity of artisanal food production optimized for its terroir. Small operations growing what fits the soil and climate can produce a surprising amount of food: *grow what grows easily*.

TV cooking programs excel at dramatic contests between chefs and the creation of elaborate dishes, but they fail to communicate the difference in taste and nutrition between factory-farmed and local produce.

The future of sustainable, affordable, nutritious food is in localized production optimized for what grows well where we live.

The satisfaction and well-being this connection with the land generates is rarely appreciated. It is not coincidental that the longest-living, healthiest groups among us--for example, the *Blue Zones* Okinawans and the Greek islanders—tend their plots of earth and their animals, and share their homegrown bounty with their families, friends and neighbors.

They enjoy a long, fulfilling life because they are productive within a small-scale, caring, sharing community—the essence of self-reliance.

Cheap Energy, Specialization and Economies of Scale

As noted earlier, our economy is optimized for specialization. We go to specialists for healthcare, auto repairs, accounting and other services. Our products are manufactured in specialized factories and shipped thousands of miles in specialized supply chains.

But the real driver of wealth over the past 200 years is cheap energy. Ever more abundant energy was a rocket-booster to specialization, transportation and the global trade of goods.

As noted previously, the easy-to-get, low-cost energy has now been extracted, and regardless of the source, energy will become increasingly costly. A great many people believe that technology will create a limitless source of low-cost energy, but these dreams ignore the limits of physics and real-world costs.

As energy become scarce and costly, economies that can only function if energy is cheap break down.

Manufacturing, transportation and trade that is only profitable if tens of millions of people buy the products and services are no longer viable. Consider the toaster. It only costs $25 because all its components are manufactured in vast quantities. As noted earlier, the cost per unit can be very low because the initial investment in production lines and the wages paid to workers are spread over a million units.

Were the factory only able to sell 1,000 units, the cost per unit would be astronomical because the initial investment is so large.

The vast majority of modern goods cannot be economically manufactured on a small scale. Thomas Thwaites attempted to make a toaster from scratch and found it was impossible to do so. He described the experience in his book, *The Toaster Project: Or a Heroic Attempt to Build a Simple Electric Appliance from Scratch*. Even the simple kitchen toaster requires highly specialized ceramics and metals that are only fabricated in a few factories.

In many cases, a handful of factories produce the entire world's supply of specialty components, solvents, etc. It simply isn't economical to produce these highly specialized components on any scale less than global.

To reduce costs, global supply chains have been streamlined down to a handful of suppliers who mass-produce products. If one component—for example, a specialty semiconductor chip—is no longer available, the entire production line is shut down.

If the products are no longer affordable to a vast number of consumers, the product line will also be shut down because it's not financially viable to operate at less than mass production.

This is why products will become increasingly unavailable. Higher costs will put products out of reach of the vast number of consumers necessary to keep economies of scale profitable. Manufacturers will shut down because they are unable to earn a profit producing fewer units, even if they raise prices. The higher the price, the fewer consumers can afford it.

If a factory only makes 1,000 toasters a year, relatively few consumers could afford the high cost of production.

Energy moves global trade, and if transportation costs rise due to higher energy costs, it has the same effect: global supply chains are only financially viable if they are moving vast quantities of goods and materials.

The same is also true in labor markets. Specialization is only profitable if a large number of consumers can afford the service. Consider a hospital with many specialist physicians and nurses. A hospital is extremely expensive to operate, and so a small population of patients can't support numerous specialists.

As economies optimized for specialization and cheap energy unravel, the economies of scale necessary to support labor specialization also unravel. As the number of jobs declines, so does the pool of consumers who can afford higher costs for products and services.

The mechanic who once had enough customers to specialize in one brand of vehicle may find there are no longer enough customers with enough money to pay specialized rates. They will have to learn how to service more types of vehicles and reduce their hourly rate to attract enough customers to support her enterprise.

In other words, specialization is only profitable if there are enormous economies of scale and millions of consumers who can afford the products. Once the pool of consumers who can afford higher prices shrinks, mass production is no longer economically viable and production shuts down.

Complexity and Dependency Chains

The complexity of modern goods is another source of system fragility. If an electronic controller fails, the device stops working. The only way to fix it is to replace the failed controller with the exact same part—there are no substitutes.

A few years ago, the controller board on our clothes dryer failed, and there was only one source: the manufacturer. The replacement controller board was about 1/4th the cost of a new dryer. Sole-source suppliers are monopolies, so they can charge whatever the market will bear. The controller boards for other brands and models won't work; you need the exact same part.

This is true of vehicles, appliances and virtually every other product with electronic components. Many products rely on sensors to function. If a single sensor fails, the product stops working. If a replacement sensor is unavailable, the product can't be repaired.

The point is that a scarcity of replacement parts means that products that fail cannot be repaired, or the repair may be extraordinarily costly.

Many essential machines require special solvents and fluids. If these are unavailable, the machines grind to a halt. For example, if Diesel Exhaust Fluid (DES) is unavailable, sensors limit diesel vehicles to a top speed of 5 miles per hour.

Institutions are also complex. If one essential process fails, the institution breaks down.

The institutions we rely on for water, food, energy, education, etc., are also dependent on economies of scale. They are like the visible peak of an iceberg above the waterline: they depend on a vast infrastructure that's invisible to most of us. As energy costs and resource scarcities melt away global economies of scale, institutions cease to function.

We're learning that scarcities can occur for many reasons: depletion, geopolitical tensions, supply chain logjams and so on.

All of these production and distribution systems are *dependency chains*: if one link in the chain breaks, the entire system grinds to a halt.

In effect, the systems we depend on are *designed to fail* in anything less than global abundance delivered by long, complex dependency chains. These systems are designed to fail because every link is a potential point of failure that can bring down the entire chain. Our global system of abundance is inherently fragile.

There are additional layers of fragility on top of scarcities and long dependency chains: the financial and Internet systems that process the billions of transactions that keep the global system of production and distribution functioning. Each of these systems has its own vulnerabilities: failures in one node can cascade, bringing down the entire system.

Scarcity, Fragility and Technological Constraints

Humans are prone to *recency bias*: we believe that the recent past is a reliable guide to the future. The past 75 years·of abundance, stability and reliable weather have lulled us into thinking that abundance, stability and good weather are permanent. We are learning these were all temporary. Though we pride ourselves on our technologies, humanity still depends on rain and soil for the majority of our food. Our technology and financial wealth cannot make unreliable weather reliable again or restore depleted aquifers and soil on a global scale.

Cheap energy, specialization and economies of scale were all optimized to expand consumption and profits. Localized production was replaced by highly profitable offshoring of production. Now the global system has been optimized to function only if energy is cheap, materials are abundant and specialized chains of production and distribution work perfectly.

We don't have to run out of energy or grain to experience crisis; anything that breaks key links in our long supply chains will disrupt the distribution of life's essentials. Grain may be in the field and oil still in the ground, but if a few links in the long supply chains break, there will be little food or fuel delivered to cities thousands of miles from the farms and oil wells.

Governments have awakened to the national security risks of dependence on foreign suppliers, and the potential for geopolitical blackmail, supply chain breakdowns and scarcities. My book on these topics is titled *Global Crisis, National Renewal* because I see a once-in-a-lifetime opportunity for national renewal in reshoring production and embracing Degrowth: *doing more with less.*

Shortening supply chains from 5,000 miles (global) to 1,500 miles (domestic) would be an advance, but 1,500-mile-long supply chains still require complex logistics and massive consumption of energy. The number of links in the dependency chains are reduced, but the vulnerabilities remain: the failure of one link still breaks the chain.

Reshoring production requires enormous investments. These will increase the costs of virtually everything. Some essentials (for example, cobalt) cannot be fully supplied domestically. The economy will still be constrained by global scarcities.

Restoring the material security of the nation will take time. There are no guarantees that scarcities can be overcome. Depletion is real and there are no substitutes for many materials.

Our modern bias is to trust technology to deliver solutions which don't require any sacrifice. We cheer all-electric pickup trucks and the successful flights of electric air taxis. When told these solutions aren't scalable due to scarcities of the materials needed to manufacture them, we insist technology will find a way. But technology isn't magic. Every technology needs materials and energy. If these are scarce and costly, technology has real-world constraints.

What happens when supply chains unravel and institutions break down? We're helpless. Most of us have few if any real-world skills and few if any personal networks built on reciprocity, trust and producing the essentials of life. Those without a foundation of self-reliance will find life much harder than those who have assembled a self-reliant way of living.

While we can hope that technology will conjure up new sources of materials and energy, it is prudent to recognize physical and financial constraints and plan accordingly. This is the heart of self-reliance: rather than count on a future techno-miracle to save us, find solutions that are within our grasp now.

The Profound Consequences of Globalization and Its Demise

Has anyone been unaffected by the hyper-globalization of the past 40 years? The answer is no. You may think *hyper-globalization* is an exaggeration, but consider that 40 years ago, not a single item in the hardware store was made in China. Now, virtually every item in the hardware store is manufactured in China. That's not merely globalization, it's hyper-globalization—near-total dependence on other nations for goods and commodities.

Consider that when the Covid pandemic hit the U.S. in 2020, there were immediate shortages of N95 masks and the precursor materials for pharmaceuticals, as the production of these (and thousands of other products) had been offshored to China to increase American corporate profits by reducing costs.

As the pandemic disrupted deliveries from Asia, U.S. auto manufacturers could not finish the assembly of vehicles due to severe shortages of semiconductors.

The consequences of hyper-globalization have not been limited to soaring corporate profits and cheaply made goods. Entire sectors of the U.S. economy have disappeared, along with hundreds of thousands of jobs. Cities that were once hubs of manufacturing and valued-added production now rely on finance, tourism, entertainment and real estate speculation for jobs and tax revenues. Meanwhile, the essential goods and commodities that support these services come from countries whose production and supply chains we don't control.

Hyper-globalization certainly boosted U.S. corporate profits, but the downside is the vulnerabilities created by relying so heavily on other nations. This dependence gives those nations the power to disrupt our economy, either as a consequence of their domestic policies—for example, China shutting down production to limit the spread of Covid—or as a way to influence our geopolitical decisions via blackmail: either support the "right" policies or suffer the consequences of being cut off from essentials.

Globalization is unraveling in real time for reasons that cannot be reversed. Every nation that depends on globalization realizes that it cuts both ways: hyper-globalization boosts exports and profits but creates vulnerabilities by giving others the power to disrupt or even cripple our economy.

Hyper-globalization has hollowed out our economy, replacing production with services and speculation, neither of which provide the material necessities of life. Financial speculation (*hyper-financialization*) has become the way to make fortunes rather than creating useful products and jobs. This dependence on speculation is not healthy, as all speculative bubbles eventually deflate, with devastating consequences.

All the low-hanging fruit of reducing costs by offshoring production has been picked, and now costs are rising regardless of where production is shipped: wages are rising globally, environmental damage must be mitigated, and depletion is causing commodity scarcities that push prices higher. Globalization is no longer a solution; it is the problem.

Will anyone be left unaffected as globalization unravels? Just as no one was left unaffected by the rise of hyper-globalization, no one will be left unaffected by its demise. On both the household and national levels, the only response that reduces our vulnerability is self-reliance.

Chapter Two: The Mindset of Self-Reliance

The Goal of Self Reliance

The goal of self-reliance is to improve well-being, security and productivity by optimizing practical skills, flexibility, trusted personal networks and what author Nassim Taleb termed *antifragility* (not just surviving adversity but emerging stronger). The purpose of increasing self-reliance is to navigate the unprecedented transition from excess consumption to securing essentials. This goal demands we avoid becoming attached to anything other than self-reliance.

Embrace Evolutionary Churn and Transparency

Self-reliance is served by understanding everything is a system, not just Nature's ecosystems but human organizations, too. When the fundamentals of life change, every ecosystem must evolve or die. This is equally true of human organizations, from households to nations.

When conditions change, this applies *selective pressure* to the system, incentivizing adaptations that work better in the new conditions. Evolution conserves what works while experimenting with mutations to find advantageous adaptations.

Nature and human systems evolve via *Natural Selection*, the process of responding to evolutionary pressures by experimenting with variations and then selecting those that are most advantageous.

In genetics and epigenetics, this process is automatic. In human organizations, those in power influence the choice of what is conserved or replaced.

Those benefiting from the system try to conserve it as is, while those weakened by selective pressure support trying something new.

Those in power have few incentives to risk changing the system, as this could undermine their power. From their perspective, evolutionary forces threaten the status quo that benefits them.

Evolution requires *transparency* and *variability*. Evolution is only possible if the system generates a steady stream of mutations / variations.

Variations are the fuel of evolution: if there are no variations, there's nothing new which might offer selective advantages.

Transparency is the mechanism needed to test variability to discover if it offers advantages.

In human organizations, transparency means there's a free-for-all churn of ideas, dissent, experimentation and sharing of results. New ideas and data flow freely between all the nodes of the system.

This free-flowing, dynamic mixing is *evolutionary churn*. Without *evolutionary churn*, systems cannot adapt. Inflexible and brittle, they break apart as all the things that no longer work chip away at the system's stability, i.e., its capacity to keep functioning.

Human organizations that lack variability and transparency fail to evolve because they lack the means to do so.

This is *scale-invariant*, meaning it's true from the smallest scale to the largest scale. Relationships, enterprises and nations lacking variability and transparency all fail for the same reasons.

Transparency is not easy. People contest our treasured orthodoxies, and we're forced to admit to being wrong more often than we like. It hurts our pride and we lose face, but the upside is the immense success of evolutionary advances generated by dissent and transparency.

Systems maintain their stability via *dynamic equilibrium*, a constant flux of variations and experiments--that is, low-level instability--continually modifying the system to maintain overall stability.

Without this constant flux of low-level instability, sources of instability pile up, unnoticed and uncorrected, until they become big enough to destabilize the entire system, causing it to crash.

In other words, the evolutionary ideal is an openness to changes that have been tested to make sure they're advantageous. When others have done the testing and they share the results, the entire group benefits.

Humans share new adaptations by communicating. This is why transparency is essential. Without it, improvements remain private rather than public.

The purpose of *dynamic equilibrium* is to maintain stability while adopting successful adaptations. If big, untested adaptations are adopted, this threatens overall stability, as the failure of the new part may destabilize the entire system.

Dynamic equilibrium is served by incremental changes rather than by a tidal wave of major changes which haven't been fully tested.

In terms of self-reliance, we don't want to undertake an armload of major changes at the same time, especially if we're not sure they'll work as intended. Throwing everything out in favor of untested changes piles up the risk that the failure in one new thing brings down our whole life.

Before we make a big change, we want to test the waters and find out what worked best for others.

We also don't want to view adaptations as threats that we must suppress because we want the status quo to continue as is. When conditions change, we can't force the existing system to work well without adapting. Clinging to what no longer works because it's been frozen in time leads to breakdown and collapse.

Suppressing variability and transparency as threats undermines the system. Evolutionary pressure doesn't go away when you hide what's no longer working; the dirty laundry piles up. When transparency and dissent are suppressed, the system has no evolutionary fuel. Starved, it collapses.

Those that encourage dissent and transparency will evolve, come what may. Those that try to force things to stay the same will fail.

This is *scale-invariant*, meaning that it works on the scale of relationships, enterprises and nations.

If dissent is suppressed, data is hoarded, communication is shackled by fear of censure and all decisions are made without any input and debate, the organization is doomed to evolutionary failure. This is true of relationships, communities, companies and nations.

The system where all the dirty laundry is out and everybody is arguing about it is evolutionarily robust. The system where the dirty laundry is hidden in the basement to preserve the illusion of unity and success has been stripped of variability and transparency. It will collapse, as the illusion of unity and success is not unity and success.

Dissent, variability, sharing ideas, proposing solutions and negotiating transparently nurture advantageous adaptations.

The self-reliant seek relationships and communities that nurture evolution and dynamic stability by welcoming new ideas and sharing what works best.

Solve Problems Ourselves

The conventional mindset depends on authorities and institutions to solve problems.

The mindset of self-reliance is direct and practical: don't just tell us the problem; tell us how you're going to fix it. We don't mean how you propose the authorities should fix it, we mean how *you're going to fix it for yourself and your household by making changes in your own life.*

We don't mean a general idea, we mean your entire plan, with each step of the process laid out including the cost in time and money, what tradeoffs are required, and your Plan B if your Plan A doesn't work as expected.

Tell us what resources, skills and help you need to see the plan through. Tell what you have on hand and how you're going to get whatever you don't yet have.

Tell us what you know and what you don't yet know but plan to learn, and how you're going to learn it. Tell us what else you've already accomplished that's similar in complexity and scale.

Tell us who you've lined up to help you and what you've already accomplished together.

The self-reliant understand that excuses, rationalizations and pie-in-the-sky proposals are all part of the human condition, but these are obstacles to real solutions and so we must set them aside in favor of focusing on practicalities.

The self-reliant understand that there are few perfect solutions. Most solutions will be contingent on things going according to plan. Any progress, however modest, Is better than no progress. Progress requires working toward a solution even if the first few attempts are failures. Small successes add up and failures are part of the learning process

Grow What Grows Easily

A useful principle of self-reliance is *Grow what grows easily and eat what grows easily*. In other words, grow whatever fits the terroir and climate where we live, and make the easy-to-grow foodstuffs the staples of our diets.

This principle applies equally well to endeavors beyond growing food: develop what's easy given our skills, enthusiasms, personalities, networks and locale. By "easy" I don't mean effortless; I mean making the necessary effort comes easier and generates more satisfaction than pursuing other options.

It takes time to learn difficult skills, but if something comes naturally and our enthusiasm makes the effort worthwhile, that's a much easier path than forcing ourselves to learn something solely because it's lucrative or expected of us.

For example, learning to play a musical instrument has a steep learning curve, i.e., the initial efforts yield paltry results. But liking the instrument makes the task much more enjoyable than being forced to learn an instrument you feel nothing for.

Grow what grows easily, and make use of what grows easily applies to the full range of self-reliance: raising food, establishing an enterprise or network, learning new skills, finding a new place to live. Nurture what will grow on its own, and make full use of what grows easily rather than depend on things that we don't control that demand much effort but yield meager results.

We Are What We Do Every Day

A useful starting-point is to ask: *what is my life optimized for*? This is different than asking what your goals are. It's a question that follows Aristotle's dictum: *We are what we repeatedly do*. In other words, regardless of what we tell ourselves or others, what we devote ourselves to every day is what we've optimized. If we're not devoting ourselves to something every day, our lives are not optimized for that; our lives are optimized for whatever we're doing every day.

For many people, the answer is "making money" because most of their time and energy is devoted to making money. For others, it's "to have fun" because they devote themselves to recreation and entertainment.

Self-reliance requires daily effort. As Emerson noted, *Do the thing and you shall have the power*." If we don't take action, our goals and aspirations remain abstractions.

Money Is Not Self-Reliance

Many people assume money makes us self-reliant. The assumption is that there will always be solutions we can buy, and so money will solve all problems. This misses the meaning of scarcity: when there is none available, there's none for sale.

Money has limits few recognize.

In real scarcities, people save what's scarce to share with those they care about. Money is secondary, because if I trade X (food, fuel, etc.) for $100, what value will that money have tomorrow? Maybe whatever I traded will be worth $200.

At some point, nobody is willing to trade scarce essentials for any amount of money, because money isn't as scarce as essentials and therefore it is of limited value.

Money can't buy what really counts: trust. Anyone who tries to buy or sell trust is untrustworthy, because they don't understand that trust isn't for sale. They will betray or cheat anyone who foolishly equates money with trust.

Money can be stolen. Trust, skills and personal networks cannot be stolen.

This is why I emphasize *trusted personal networks* as a foundation of self-reliance. Networks of trust and personal bonds (starting with family) were the foundation of global trading networks for thousands of years. In the modern era, we trust institutions to act as neutral clearing houses for transactions. But as institutions become unreliable, then *trusted personal networks* regain their importance.

Self-Reliance Is Not Self-Sufficiency

One of America's iconic images is the self-sufficient frontier household. But this is a myth, not reality. Every household, not matter how much they provide for themselves, still relies on industrial production of glass containers, plastics, tools, connectors, wire, lubricants, fuels, fabrics, sealants, solvents, gaskets, O-rings, medications, etc., as well as the Internet, electrical grid, roadways, healthcare and other infrastructure. In the digital age, communications depend on complex mobile phones constructed of highly specialized components.

Equipment such as generators and systems such as heat pumps, solar arrays and wind turbines are all made of components that are impossible to make without specialized materials and equipment.

The mindset of self-reliance understands self-sufficiency is always partial, but that reducing our need for industrial products and acquiring equipment that will last a long time and is repairable, are key strategies of self-reliance. The goal of self-reliance isn't to live without any industrial products. The goal of self-reliance is to be close to sources of essentials and seek the most durable, easy-to-repair equipment that enable us to consume the least amount possible and be as productive as possible.

Super-Abundance Is Unsustainable

The self-reliant understand that the belief that finance runs the world is an illusion generated by abundance. In reality, energy is the foundation of modern life. The self-reliant understand the global economy is a system which is no longer sustainable, and this system lacks the means to successfully adapt to scarcity, i.e., *degrowth*.

The mindset of self-reliance understands that the seemingly limitless cheap energy and resources that powered an ever-expanding super-abundance are limited, and so the *waste is growth Landfill Economy* is no longer sustainable.

There won't be enough resources to expand consumption. What resources and energy that are available must be devoted to maintaining the industrial base, leaving little for discretionary consumption.

If we don't ration essentials such as fuel and food, the wealthy will buy up whatever is available and the rest of the populace won't be able to afford to live. That will trigger social disorder and the overthrow of regimes.

The Appeal of Denial, Wishful Thinking and Rationalization

The mindset of self-reliance understands that humans resolve uncertainty by rationalizing ways to avoid difficult choices. The self-reliant set aside rationalizations as unproductive. The self-reliant base their forecast on realistic assessments, and do not waste time and energy arguing about rationalizations. Events will prove one perspective is realistic and the rest are not. Those who cling to rationalizations will be served a much different banquet of consequences than the self-reliant.

The mindset of self-reliance accepts being wrong and adjusting accordingly. If the forecast of systemic scarcity is wrong and super-abundance continues, that won't negate self-reliance, which increases well-being and productivity. But if those forecasting permanent abundance are wrong, they will be woefully unprepared for scarcity.

Author Nassim Taleb pointed out the key difference between those who seek to rationalize wishful thinking, and those who seek realistic assessments. The conclusions of those clinging to rationalizations never waver. No matter what new information is presented, their conclusion remains the same. The evidence-based processes of the realists never waver, but their conclusions change with new information.

For example, if additional evidence of energy scarcity is presented, the rationalizers' conclusion—that energy is inherently abundant and all we need to do is tap it with new technology—never changes. There is always some bit of news about a technological break-through to support their conclusion. The practicality, cost and timeline for this breakthrough to replace the existing energy system is left unaddressed.

Those applying a realistic problem-solving method focus on the practicalities the rationalizers studiously avoid: how much will this new technology cost? What materials does it require? Are there enough of these materials to enable a global expansion of this technology? What are the environmental and maintenance costs? What are the *opportunity costs* of investing in this new technology, i.e., where else could we have invested the capital and gained a higher return?

The rationalizers are annoyed by these questions. The solution in their minds is to hold fast to whatever wishful-thinking relieves their anxieties about a potentially difficult future.

The self-reliant understand that the desire to avoid sacrifices is part of the human condition. They understand that the discipline required to analyze problems in a practical manner is not natural, as it requires embracing uncertainty rather than avoiding it. This process must be learned like any other skill, through practice.

Holding fast to wishful-thinking ("it will all work out by itself") does not actually solve problems in the real world. Rather, rationalizations are obstacles to real-world solutions, as real solutions require accepting uncertainty and difficult tradeoffs.

The self-reliant understand that looking at problems in the contexts of systems and enterprises helps us identify the inputs, processes and outputs (systems thinking), and costs, revenues, constraints and tradeoffs (entrepreneurial thinking).

The self-reliant understand that *everyone's life is a system and an enterprise*, whether we think about it in those terms or not.

Constraints, Tradeoffs and Triage

Goals are important, but the self-reliant understand that solutions must work within constraints, and that every solution requires tradeoffs.

The American mythology holds that the limits that hold us back are of imagination: there are no limits if we dream big enough. Everything becomes possible once we leave small goals and thinking behind.

What we think certainly limits our options. We can visualize this as a circle. Inside the circle is what we think could be changed and outside the circle is what we think can't be changed.

In a geographic analogy, if we can't leave a place, then our options are narrowed to moving to a nearby neighborhood. If where we can live includes the entire world, our options expand accordingly.

But "no limits" thinking still has to operate in the constraints of our situation—and every situation has constraints. If our "no limits" goal is to make it big as a music group, we must buy instruments and learn to play them, schedule gigs, record our own songs, build a fan base online—all the laborious steps required to reach fame and fortune.

If our goal is to become more self-reliant, then we have to start with what's possible (i.e., within reach) and figure out how much each option will cost in time, money and effort, and what sacrifices or tradeoffs we'll have to make.

Every goal has an *opportunity cost*, meaning that whatever it costs in time and money could have been invested in another project. This tradeoff requires careful study.

What are the odds of success of each project? Could this project become a money-pit that swallows all our capital? Would we be better off investing in a longer-term project with big payoffs, or investing in small projects we can manage more easily?

In our initial enthusiasm, we may brush off obstacles that end up dragging the project to a halt. We may underestimate costs because we don't want to conclude "it can't be done." We may overestimate our ability to see the project through and dismiss sacrifices that become more painful than we'd imagined.

Few of us have perfect knowledge of a project before we start. We don't yet know what we don't know, and so it's impossible to anticipate every potential difficulty. A little ignorance is to be expected, but a great deal of ignorance sets up disillusionment.

We might reassess what "can't be changed:" where we live, our career, etc. After a particularly trying day, we might ask, "Why do I have to stay in this job? Isn't there any way we can get by on less income?"

In other words, we might question the constraints that we once accepted as unchangeable and conclude that, rather than being unchangeable, *they have to change*.

Triage is the process of prioritizing care to those most in need. In terms of constraints and tradeoffs, it means we can't do everything we might want to do, and we can't save everything in our current life if we're transitioning to a more self-reliant way of living.

Triage means letting go of what we can't save, or can't save without sacrificing opportunities for much more valuable advances. Triage is often painful, as we have to accept the limits of our time, money and effort and prioritize our goals to what we can realistically manage. Trying to do too much may end up accomplishing little if our resources are scattered over too many projects.

Triage means ruthlessly prioritizing and setting everything else— including things we previously considered vital—aside.

At the top of the list of priorities is our own health. As I emphasize in my book on burnout (*When You Can't Go On: Burnout, Reckoning and Renewal*), if we burn out due to overwork or chronic stress, we're no longer able to do much for ourselves or others. It's the equivalent of running out of water in an unforgiving desert.

As we prioritize, we want to leave ourselves room to maneuver, what my fellow author Mark Jeftovic calls *optionality*. In his words, "he who has the most options, usually wins." Optionality means avoiding situations that are difficult or impossible to reverse. When piloting a small aircraft, we don't want to fly into a narrow box canyon where there's not enough air space to turn around.

In other words, to keep our options open, we need to avoid committing everything we have to situations with no way to say, "this isn't working, let's choose another option."

Preserving optionality is served by breaking problems into their most fundamental parts, a process of identifying *first principles* and then working from there.

First principles are the bedrock we build on. In science, these are the fundamentals of nature: gravity, electromagnetism, etc. In our lives, they're who we are, the principles we live by, our skills and our current circumstances.

In decision-making, the principles are making realistic assessments of priorities and tradeoffs and ways to preserve optionality.

For example, if we're moving to a new locale, if we immediately buy an expensive property, we've boxed ourselves into a situation that's not easy to reverse. A better choice in terms of preserving optionality would be a rent month-to-month until we've fully scouted the new environment.

Charting the Easier Path

I already mentioned the principle of *grow what's easy to grow*. Two related ideas are *ease of flow* and *power relations*. What's easy given what we have on hand? What path has fewer obstacles? This is *ease of flow*. If we choose a path where every step requires monumental effort (i.e., very little ease of flow), reaching our goal becomes far more problematic.

Here's an analogy from nature. If we want to start a garden and we pick a patch of infertile soil, it's going to take a lot of time and effort to build the soil up to being productive. If we pick a plot with rich soil, it will be much easier to start a productive garden.

Power relations are defined by these questions: whose permission do I need to move forward? Who could obstruct me from reaching my goal? Who's help do I need that I can't do without? In other words, who has the power to help or obstruct?

Here's an example. Let's say you want to buy a property and start a new business. If you're married, you'll need the approval of your spouse. If you need to borrow money, you'll need the permission of a lender. If the business needs a license, you'll need the permission of the local government.

The fewer permissions you need to proceed and the fewer potential obstacles, the easier the path.

Discipline and Judgement

If we haven't carefully thought through a course of action, should it fall apart, we're prone to disorganization. In that frame of mind, it's easy to make decisions we later regret. If we haven't practiced preparing a backup plan, we're not going to learn how when we're under pressure. We need to practice beforehand.

This process requires discipline and self-control. Being able to recognize that we're not at our best is critical when we're exhausted. Recognizing that our ability to make good decisions is impaired is a critical skill, as the awareness that we may be making a mistake helps us avoid getting trapped in even worse circumstances.

It's easy to overestimate our experience and judgment. If the situation is novel, our experience may not be a sufficient guide. We like to think of ourselves as strong and resourceful, but it's useful to recognize our limits and not count on reserves we may no longer have.

Being decisive can be advantageous, but only after a process of deliberation. Colonel John Boyd's *OODA loop* (Observe, Orient, Decide, Act) is instructive: better to take the time to observe, orient what's happening in the appropriate context, figure out how best to preserve optionality, recognize we might be making a mistake, and then chart a course of action.

I've learned the hard way that my judgement decays rapidly when I'm burned out. Maintaining discipline and self-control is the means to avoid rash actions.

Insight isn't entirely rational. After thinking through a situation, we may experience an intuitive insight that synthesizes everything we've observed, felt and pondered.

The wider our experience and the more we've practiced these analytic processes, the higher the odds our assessments will be helpful. The more we know about our own limits, the higher the odds our judgements will be practical.

If we haven't been pushed to our limits, we may not realize how much risk we're taking on and how close to the edge we've come.

A tragic example of this is the California couple who went on a day hike with their young child and dog. They were experienced hikers in excellent physical condition, but they did not bring enough water as they'd never experienced extreme temperatures in a barren, rugged terrain. It seems they hadn't experienced the first stages of heat prostration and did not recognize the danger. As a result, they were unable to recognize the risk they faced or the *point of no return* when dehydration and overheating spiral into fatal heat stroke.

We may think we're experienced and know what we're doing, but extreme conditions are not the same as ordinary conditions. Our experience of everyday life does not necessarily prepare us for recognizing points of no return in more challenging conditions.

When we're out of our depth, we're prone to latching on to wishful thinking or past experiences which are not appropriate guides in more adverse conditions. We may be tempted to think that if we just press on, we'll succeed by virtue of pressing on. But persevering is not all that's needed to succeed. The plan has to be appropriate to the conditions and the limits of our resources.

In my experience, we don't understand the risks of the sea until we're close to drowning. We don't understand the risks of ladders and heights until we fall. We don't understand thirst until we're woozy from dehydration. We don't understand how our judgement can be impaired until we're disoriented. We don't understand the difference between an investment and a gamble until we've lost our entire nest egg.

I've experienced all of these and been lucky to escape without life-threatening injuries or losses I couldn't survive. In many cases, it was a close thing. As a result, risk and the limits of my resources and experience are ever-present in my mind.

It's fine to take risks, but we have to know what they are before we take the first step. The problem is risk tends to remain invisible until it's too late.

Maintaining a Margin of Safety

You've probably noted the overlap of *self-reliance* and *resilience*, the capacity to survive adversity. The self-reliant household strengthens resilience by reducing fragilities and vulnerabilities in basic ways. For example, the self-reliant avoid putting all the household's eggs in one basket by diversifying skills, networks, incomes and assets.

Another basic resilience strategy is to maintain a margin of safety so that a crisis doesn't cripple our ability to respond. Examples include stored food and water, a water filter, emergency lighting, etc. Financially, having cash and savings is a margin of safety.

In the analogy of hiking in rugged, barren terrain, carrying extra water is a margin of safety. So is carefully conserving whatever water is remaining so there's some left for the last push to safety.

Chronic stress is a form of adversity that's difficult to measure or control, and so we may lose sight of the need to maintain a margin of safety in our physical and psychological strength.

Once we run out of water. money or our core strength, life becomes much more precarious.

Plans A, B and C

Mike Tyson memorably described the need for Plan B when Plan A doesn't work as anticipated: "Everybody has a plan until they get hit." (This quote is also attributed as "Everybody has a plan until they get punched in the mouth.") In other words, when our first plan breaks down, we freeze up because we don't have a backup plan.

Life is full of unexpected hits: losing a job, accidents, medical emergencies, financial losses, businesses failing, relationship breakups and more.

Many of these hits are temporary setbacks. Others change the entire context of our lives. It's one thing to lose a job and find another similar one, it's another when the entire industry our livelihood depended on crumbles. If we burn out, we may not be able to resume our previous workload. Grandparents or grandchildren may join our household. If our neighborhood no longer feels safe, that's not going to change overnight. If we suffer catastrophic financial losses, there is no reset button that restores what was lost.

Life-changing events reorder our constraints and force a reappraisal of our priorities and resources (i.e., triage).

Realizing that our Plan A may break on contact with a fast-changing world opens opportunities to increase our self-reliance with basic planning.

I have often suggested a simple formula for methodically planning a range of responses ahead of time so we're ready when and if our circumstances change: Plans A, B and C.

Plan A is our response should our circumstances change while the socio-economic system and our life situation (health, relationships, finances) all remain pretty much the same. An example might be unexpectedly losing your job due to a recession and being unable to find a replacement job in the same field at the same wage.

Plan B is our response should our circumstances change while the system and/or our circumstances are decaying. An example might be we no longer feel safe in our neighborhood due to rising crime and a dysfunctional local government.

Plan C is our response should the socio-economic system break down around us. An example might be supply chains fail and gas stations no longer have fuel and grocery store shelves are empty. Whether such a breakdown will be temporary or chronic is unknowable, so we have to be prepared for both possibilities.

No matter how unlikely a breakdown might be, the consequences are so dire that it's prudent to prepare a response. Making a plan ahead of time requires no money and only a modest amount of effort. Trying to figure out what to do in a chaotic crisis rarely leads to good results. More typically, trying to figure out what to do when we're overwhelmed leads to poor decisions that may worsen the situation.

Common sense suggests preparing a plan that avoids adversity as much as possible rather than waiting until adversity has reached maximum disruptive force.

The act of writing down all the assumptions being made in Plan A ("everything will work out without us having to make any sacrifices or changes") helps us realize just how vulnerable our Plan A is to disruption.

Another benefit of preparing Plans A, B and C is that we may conclude that there is much to be gained by taking action before a crisis rather than waiting until the crisis washes ashore. By then, our options will have significantly narrowed.

Optionality is only useful if we take action before the options disappear.

For example, trying to leave a city when everyone else is trying to leave will only trap us in gridlock. Our Plans B and C should be designed to get us out of the city a week, month or even a year before the crisis arrives.

Systems unravel unpredictably and unevenly. Some locales may remain relatively stable while many unravel and others break down. Some forms of wealth may gain value while others become worthless. Things we assume will always be available may become unavailable.

Living and working in a productive community that values our contributions offers advantages that cannot be matched by money alone. What we assume is our biggest asset—wealth—may slip away or even become a liability by becoming a target.

Towing an Iceberg

When we're young, we can load all our earthly possessions in a beat-up car and beeline to a new circumstance. It's especially easy if we're not tied to a job and aren't responsible for taking care of anyone but ourselves.

For example, in our early 20s we moved everything we owned in a compact car. We arrived with no job or prospects other than an offer to build a plywood micro-house on a friend's rural acreage without electricity or water. We camped onsite while building the 12-foot by 16-foot dwelling with hand tools. Moving into the barebones plywood shelter felt luxurious.

Later in life, it's not so easy. My analogy is we're *towing an iceberg*: 90% of what we're pulling isn't readily visible but it's most of the weight. When we're responsible for others, have a household of possessions, higher standards of comfort and much heavier financial obligations, there is much more to do to make big changes. The paperwork alone is an iceberg: obtaining new insurance and drivers licenses, finding dentists and doctors, filing new business licenses, opening new bank / credit union accounts, changing addresses in online accounts, registering children in new schools, locating senior centers for live-in parents and so on.

Changing careers is demanding, and so is downsizing spending. Major changes such as moving put tremendous stress on relationships and households.

Our health might constrain us in ways we never anticipated in our youth. Once we're burned out, for example, how much we can accomplish every day is limited.

The consensus in our relationships and household may fragment and we may have to renegotiate our approach to our new circumstances. Unexpected disappointments may arise. For example, the house and property that was purchased with such enthusiasm may require months of tedious, costly repairs we did not fully anticipate.

Understanding that we'll be towing an iceberg doesn't make the task any easier, but it does help us prepare for difficulties and disappointments. Laying out our constraints, tradeoffs and Plans A, B and C will help us assess the true size of the iceberg we'll be towing.

Reducing Complexity

Modern life is complex, and adversity adds additional obstacles. Anything we can do to reduce complexity reduces the pressures on us.

The conventional approach to reducing complexity is to automate whatever can be automated, for example, setting up autopay for utilities bills. This is helpful but not everything can be automated. It's useful to differentiate between *self-organizing complexity* and complexity that must be micro-managed every step of the way.

One analogy is a home garden. If the garden is tidy rows of the same vegetable, it must be weeded and attention must be paid to insect infestations. This is a care-intensive garden.

The alternative approach is planting a messy-looking garden of various vegetables and herbs that isn't as demanding as tidy rows. This order is largely self-organized. If the plants are selected to complement each other, the diversity benefits all the plants and the gardener, as there is little bare ground to fill with weeds and the diversity reduces insect infestations.

One of my favorite sayings given to me by my friend S.T. is "don't mess with my mess." What looks like a disorganized tabletop of tools, nails and paint cans is a workplace that doesn't need any further organization. It's low-maintenance complexity.

No enterprise is entirely self-organizing, but some are easier to operate than others. Micro-managing every step consumes a lot of time and energy, and it's not *fault-tolerant*, meaning once you take your attention elsewhere, the whole thing falls apart. Other types of complexity are more fault-tolerant; they will pretty much run on their own with occasional oversight, like the messy garden.

The most burdensome parts of the iceberg we're towing are the fault-intolerant complexities that require a lot of time and energy to keep them functioning.

Recognizing the more demanding kinds of complexity and trying to break them down into less demanding processes or eliminating them entirely improves self-reliance.

Humans readily adapt to new circumstances and stop questioning whether everything is still necessary. The self-reliant understand the value of asking these basic questions: is this really necessary, or do I just think it's necessary because I've grown accustomed to it? If I had to do without this, would it matter? What else could I do with my time and energy if this task disappeared? Do I enjoy doing this or is it a burden?

Sometimes complexity serves an important purpose, for example, accounting. Other times, it just increases the stress in our lives with little payoff. Reducing that kind of complexity increases our self-reliance.

We Control Completion, not Success

In my experience, self-reliance is furthered by understanding the difference between completion of a project and the success we envisioned. We control completion, not success as it's generally understood.

We can complete a creative endeavor, but we can't control whether it's successful in terms of recognition, praise or financial rewards.

If we renovate a house, we can complete the project but we can't control the future market value of the property.

We can launch a new enterprise but we can't guarantee its financial success.

We can move somewhere but we can't be sure it will check every box of what we define as successful.

All we can do is complete projects. That's the only form of success we control.

Cooperation Is Security

In the U.S., "solutions" is a code-word for something designed to reap a profit. Profit-generating "solutions" are aimed at consumers. The reality that many solutions require cooperation is ignored because what's profitable is framing "solutions" in the context of the consumer buying products and services.

Products are not the solutions they're touted to be for the simple reason that individual consumers do not live in a vacuum. As systems unravel, solutions require cooperation.

In the conventional mindset, security is served by households buying supplies. Having a well-stocked larder is an important Plan B strategy, but in the long run, self-reliance demands producing essentials, not just stockpiling them to get through a few weeks or months.

Production requires cooperation. No individual, no matter how well equipped, can match the security and productive potential of a close-knit group. Humans have lived in groups since time immemorial because cooperation provides security that isolated individuals can't match.

Cooperation is the ultimate source of humanity's evolutionary success. Self-reliance is served by both individual effort and by participating in trusted networks of people who look out for each other. In military terms, this is called *unit cohesion*. There is no substitute for producing, cooperating and caring, and so building trusted networks is the core goal of self-reliance. Caring about others is the core of trusted personal networks.

Self-reliance seeks ways to cooperate rather than sources of conflict. If someone is fair, honest, trustworthy (i.e., someone who does what they said they were going to do), generous and productive, their political or religious beliefs and affiliations are not relevant to our cooperation. The conventional mindset seeks reasons why we can't cooperate, i.e., sources of conflict, because these attract social media audiences.

Self-reliance is based not on abstract loyalties but on trusted personal networks of honest, trustworthy, productive, generous individuals.

The Source of Our Self-Worth

Human societies are competitive because those who gain higher social status have more opportunities for marriage, wealth and power. Given this set of incentives, the natural source of self-worth is how we're doing in the competition for higher social status.

In the era of social media, we gain self-worth by boosting our visibility online. We pursue this goal by posting flattering images exotic travels, lavish meals, etc. These curated posts present an idealized digital avatar worthy of the admiration of others.

How do we feel good about ourselves? Certainly, by becoming accomplished, but also by being seen as attractive, popular, influential and wealthy. Would our self-worth be the same if no one knew about our accomplishments? If our successes exist only in private, do we feel as good about ourselves as when we're publicly lauded? For most of us, much of our self-worth is dependent on the recognition and approval of others.

The self-reliant have a different approach to self-worth.

That we all want to share our success is human nature, so the self-reliant want to share their advances, too. But since self-reliance is the opposite of the conspicuous consumption and self-glorification that gains conventional approval, self-reliance doesn't lend itself to public display. Not only is self-reliance based on consuming less rather than more, it is also about reducing dependency—in this case, dependency on the approval of others.

Many of the key attributes of self-reliance are internal. There's nothing to share publicly because there's nothing visible to photograph.

Boosting self-worth via competing for the recognition of others doesn't work for self-reliance. The self-reliant don't compete for others' approval, they only compete with themselves to become more self-reliant. This competition is private. Improving self-reliance is a personal accomplishment, not a public event.

Not only does self-reliance not boost social status, pursuing the approval of others distracts from self-reliance. Self-reliance reduces dependencies, and to the degree that our self-worth is dependent on the approval of others, that pursuit reduces our self-reliance.

The self-reliant draw upon internal sources of self-worth. There isn't any upside to depending on the approval of others for our self-worth, as that approval is superficial.

We don't control the opinions of others. We do control our internal sources of self-worth.

The self-reliant prefer low profiles and low visibility, as high visibility can become a liability. The self-reliant prefer to be ordinary and unworthy of notice. The self-reliant prefer to be of no interest to those outside their trusted personal networks.

The self-reliant mindset views the world differently than the conventional mindset. The goals, priorities and sources of purpose, meaning and self-worth are all different. Success is private rather than broadcast, as broadcasting an idealized version of ourselves does not improve self-reliance.

True Wealth Cannot Be Bought; The Joys of Mastery and Sharing

Self-reliance boils down to acquiring the skills to do for ourselves and our trusted network what we once relied on others to do. The joy of accomplishment and sharing is the heart of self-reliance: being able to do more for ourselves and those we care about is rewarding.

Accomplishing real world tasks that help those we care about provides a satisfaction that cannot be duplicated with money-status accomplishments that our culture considers so valuable: making more money, getting a fancier title, etc.

This may sound like Zen koans, but in my experience *true wealth is mastery freely shared*, and with *true mastery is no small thing done badly*.

In the mindset of self-reliance, making more money and having higher status don't qualify as accomplishments unless there is mastery of real-world skills. True accomplishment is mastery (*no small thing done badly*) and true wealth is *mastery freely shared*.

Mastery is not a brand, nor is it exclusive. It is not perfection; it is simply *no small thing done badly*. Mastery is open to everyone.

In the global economy optimized to maximize profits, low quality is hidden behind a glossy exterior. Many small things are done badly to increase profits. When one shoddy component fails, the entire device fails.

The conventional mindset of maximizing profits by cutting corners has no place for mastery.

The development of true mastery and the sharing of this mastery with others is real accomplishment and real wealth.

This wealth cannot be bought because it is reserved for participants, not consumers. It is only as a participant that we can enjoy freely shared mastery.

Here is an example of mastery (*no small thing done badly*), true wealth, sharing and joy.

Like many people, we've often invited those far from home to our Thanksgiving meals. On one such occasion, we had two dozen people in our small two-bedroom apartment. One of the guests was in town to apprentice at a famous restaurant known for its farm-to-table philosophy and the artful simplicity of its seasonal cuisine. I felt embarrassed to ask such a talented chef to make the mashed potatoes and gravy but she was enthusiastic about helping with such simple dishes.

With a half-dozen people already busy in our tiny kitchen, she ended up outside, working on our concrete patio.

Her mashed potatoes and gravy were revelations, far above anything I'd ever tasted before. They weren't fancy, they were just incredibly good. I realized that for her, *no small thing was done badly*. Even the simplest dish, mashed potatoes, was prepared with care.

None of the other guests even knew who prepared the mashed potatoes. Getting recognition isn't the goal of mastery.

As a construction worker from the age of 19 and later as a builder, I was always under time and money pressure to get the work done as fast and cleanly as possible. Self reliance is different. Yes, time, efficiency and cost matter. But so do the joys of mastery and sharing.

Chapter Three: The Nuts and Bolts of Self-Reliance

Here is my list of the nuts and bolts of self-reliance.

These are distilled from my experience. I am average in self-reliance, aptitudes and skills. I present this list not as someone on the peak looking down but as someone on the trail looking up. Self-reliance is a work in progress, not a destination.

These are guidelines that have helped me, but everyone has to chart their own course. As Emerson explained, the essence of self-reliance is that each individual makes their own assessments, decisions and plans, based on their unique circumstances. These are general principles. My hope is that some will be useful to you.

1. Get healthy and stay healthy.
2. Cultivate the inner strengths described by Emerson: to think independently and not be swayed by conformity or the opinions of others; rely on ourselves, trust our intuition and take action: *"Do the thing and you shall have the power."*
3. Cooperation and reciprocity: becoming a productive participant in a trusted network of people producing and procuring essentials.
4. Focus on producing and sharing rather than taking.
5. Finding solutions for ourselves and our households rather than relying on authorities.
6. Need less, consume less, waste nothing. Become resourceful.
7. Reduce dependency on fragile supply chains and energy-intensive systems.
8. Be flexible. Thomas Z. Zhang's translation of Chapter 76 of the *Tao Te Ching* offers a succinct summary: *"Rigidity leads to death, flexibility results in survival."* My old philosophy professor, Chang Chung-yuan, translated the following line as: *"Thus, when troops are inflexible, they lose the war."*
9. Pursue projects that can be completed with the resources we have on hand. As Sun Tzu put it: *"If a battle cannot be won, do not fight it."*

10. Be willing to move to places with fewer institutional rigidities, fewer dependencies on global supply chains and more local sources of essentials.
11. Develop practical, experiential skills to produce basic goods and services.
12. Accumulate all forms of capital, tangible and intangible. These are the foundation of self-reliance.
13. Develop self-knowledge of our strengths and constraints, and the ability to be realistic in assessments and decisions.
14. Develop a working knowledge of systems: we live within systems, and our life can best be understood as a system.
15. Become antifragile, which means navigating adversity and emerging with greater strength and adaptability.
16. Seek a diversity of interests, skills, networks, incomes and assets; all our eggs should not be in one basket. This reduces fragility and boosts adaptability.
17. Gain control of as much of your life as possible. Own your skills, work, assets, health, enterprises, interests, networks and integrity.
18. Self-reliance is not a destination we reach; it is a process of dynamic evolution as we respond to challenges in the here and now and those we see on the path ahead.

Again, everyone's path to greater self-reliance is unique. We can't just follow someone else's path to greater self-reliance. The first step to becoming more self-reliant is to chart our own path. That is the essence of self-reliance.

Get Healthy, Stay Healthy

Let's start with the most fundamental essential, health. If our health—physical, emotional, cognitive or psychological—is impaired, our self-reliance is also impaired, as we're simply not able to get as much done as we could if we were healthy.

The ideal state of health is to be healthy without medications or dietary / fitness extremes. If it takes extraordinary effort to be healthy, that cuts out the majority of people. This can't be the case, as humans have evolved to maintain health with ordinary diets and fitness.

Health is less a precarious state requiring extraordinary effort and more a matter of avoiding detrimental habits by turning common-sense routines of eating real foods and basic fitness into daily habits.

The self-reliant maintain *strength, endurance, flexibility and agility* because these physical attributes enable us to get more done. These attributes require sustained effort but not extreme effort.

Our economy focuses on selling products and services to consumers. Advertising and PR constantly promote the idea that we can achieve glowing, attractive health if we buy corporate products and services. Many people end up focusing on diet, as if diet is the only key to health. But fitness is just as important as diet. We don't need corporate products to be healthy, we simply need real food grown in nutrient-rich soil. We don't need a gym to be fit, we simply need sustained effort on basic fitness. Any six-foot-by-six-foot (two-meter by two-meter) area is enough to maintain fitness. No equipment is necessary.

The *Blue Zones* populations who remain healthy and active in their 90s are not healthy because they take handfuls of supplements or work out in a home gym; they're healthy because they eat real food that they grow themselves and are physically and socially active.

In terms of maintaining a diet of real foods, we're up against corporations that spend millions of dollars engineering products to hijack our pleasure centers via heavy doses of salt, sweetness and fat, all of which are relatively rare in the natural world but common in designed-to-be-addictive snacks, meals and fast-food.

The simple strategy is to avoid all corporate products and stick with real foods.

While there is a broad range of opinions about food, we have living examples of what constitutes a healthy diet and fitness routine: the *Blue Zones* people have diets rich in nutrients, fiber, variety and moderation, and lifestyles rich in purpose, sharing, social connections and productive labor caring for their gardens and animals.

These groups don't pursue extremes of dietary restrictions or punishing fitness routines, but they live a long time and are able to work productively into very advanced ages.

All the people I know who are still healthy at 90+ years of age share one trait: they are physically active. They take a daily walk and work in their yard. Many studies have found that physical activity improves well-being and mental acuity at all ages.

Unfortunately, fitness is often perceived as demanding extremes that exceed what many of us can manage. As a general rule, simple stretching, walking and brief exertions to maintain heart and lung capacity and muscle mass are enough to maintain fitness. For example, studies have found that walking 4,000 steps a day provides a basic level of fitness.

The goal of fitness is to be able to maintain our health, do physical work and enjoy an active life. The other goal is to maintain the capacity to overcome adversity, for example, being able to swim or walk far enough to reach safety.

Self-reliance requires an ability to sort the wheat from the chaff when presented with medical claims that are highly profitable to those promoting the claims.

Marginally beneficial medications with many side effects can be presented positively via sleight-of-hand statistics and positive reviews by healthcare professionals whose financial gains from promoting the product are carefully obscured. Research that is presented as objective may be funded by a corporation which stands to benefit from positive results.

Addictive snacks, fast food, medications, alcohol, drugs, pornography, gambling, etc. are highly profitable. Freeing ourselves of addictions is arduous. We fear losing a coping mechanism that despite its terrible consequences relieved some of our anxiety, depression, loneliness, purposelessness, post-traumatic suffering, etc.

Self-reliance is served by substituting productive coping mechanisms that we control for destructive addictions we don't control.

Chronic stress impairs our health. Finding ways to limit chronic stress is a core topic in my book on burnout, *When You can't Go On: Burnout, Reckoning and Renewal.*

Health is our ultimate source of well-being and self-reliance. If our health is impaired by destructive habits and dependencies, our self-reliance will also be impaired. When we need our full powers, we may find ourselves unable to respond.

As Lao Tzu reminds us, being flexible is advantageous: *"The big and rigid would be overtaken by the nimble and flexible."*

Being self-reliant takes sustained effort. If we're not healthy, we lack the means to be as productive as we could be.

Cultivate Independence in Thought and Action

For Emerson, the essence of self-reliance is to think independently and cultivate the inner strength to be ourselves rather than conform to others' expectations. This is difficult because humans are social animals highly attuned to our status in the group. We want to be accepted, and fear being shunned.

If we take a well-worn path to gain approval, we cannot succeed in being our best selves, for that requires pursuing our own enthusiasms.

Success for the self-reliant isn't defined solely by financial wealth or the approval of others. Success is defined by becoming our best selves by pursuing our enthusiasms in productive, resourceful ways.

We become our best selves by taking action: as Emerson counseled, *"Do the thing and you shall have the power."*

Productive Participation in a Trusted Network

Among the many things that can't be bought, two of the most important are integrity and trust, i.e., completing what we said we were going to do in a competent, timely manner.

Small businesses are networks of trust and integrity by necessity. Small enterprises fail when suppliers and subcontractors don't get the job done on time and on budget. People who can't complete what they promised are toxic to small business, and so we quickly identify trusted suppliers and subcontractors. Those who accept the low bid from an unknown bidder risk losing their business should that bidder be incompetent or dishonest.

This model has been the foundation of enterprise for thousands of years. Trading voyages from ancient Rome to India, for example, were largely family enterprises based on trusted ship captains, contacts in ports and suppliers along trade routes.

Cooperation is based on mutual benefit and reciprocity: helping your enterprise is beneficial for my enterprise. If I vouch for someone and that person fails to do what was promised, trust in my judgment drops within my network. As a result, I won't vouch for anyone who hasn't proven themselves worthy of trust.

In other words, the trusted network provides financial benefits to every participant by vouchsafing the integrity and trust of each participant.

Corporations expand far beyond trusted networks by substituting military-style hierarchies of accountability and authority: subordinates who fail to perform are replaced.

But networks of trust pervade the corporate world as well. Executives and board members are typically recruited via trusted networks, many of which have roots in universities and community organizations.

Trusted networks don't have to be formal enterprises. They can be informal neighborhood, social or family-based networks based on reciprocity: everyone shares what they have in surplus. If something is given, something will be given in return. This is integrity in action.

Who will get first dibs on essential goods and services? Those contributing to the well-being of everyone in the network, or a stranger waving a wad of cash? Those who choose the stranger waving cash over a member of the network will have sacrificed their most valuable assets and the most important requirements of membership; integrity, reciprocity and trust.

Producing and Sharing Rather than Taking

Given a choice between taking and producing and sharing, the self-reliant will choose producing and sharing. Taking is easy but it encourages entitlement and dependence, the opposite of self-reliance.

Aiding those who cannot care for themselves—children, the elderly, the disabled and the ill—is the hallmark of civil society. But the system must balance available resources with needs. If costs are open-ended but resources are not, the system is unsustainable and will break down.

This is the problem with current healthcare and pension plans: the costs are open-ended but the resources are limited. The plans were based on projections of there always being four workers to support each retiree and an economy that always expands at the same rate as the costs of healthcare and pensions.

But as the birthrate has declined and people live longer, the worker-retiree ratio has fallen to less than two workers for every retiree, and healthcare costs have risen from a modest share of the economy to almost 20% of the economy.

The incentive in America's healthcare system is to maximize profits by selling more healthcare to insurers and government programs such as Medicaid and Medicare. There are no limits on how much these programs cost, so the costs are rising by leaps and bounds while the economy paying the bills is stagnating for all the reasons described in Chapter One.

The expedient fix has been to borrow trillions of dollars to pay for programs with no limits on cost. Borrowing from tomorrow to spend more today is only sustainable if there are unlimited resources available tomorrow. Resources are finite, so the future will have fewer resources, not more.

This mismatch of open-ended costs and limited resources is politically untouchable because people expect whatever they were promised to be fulfilled. They don't want to hear the promises they were given cannot be met.

Rather than accept that the promises that were made decades ago are no longer realistic, we borrow from the future to consume more today. This is not sustainable. Trying to keep promises of ever-expanding entitlements will break the system. One way or another, costs and resources will come into balance. Promises that cannot be kept will be broken.

As I've described in my blog posts, the only way to distribute resources fairly is rationing, so everyone gets a minimum of food, fuel and other resources. Whether this is politically acceptable is an open question.

We all understand the feeling of entitlement: other people got what they were promised, why should I be denied what I was promised?

Self-reliance requires setting the feelings of entitlement aside in favor of navigating a world with fewer resources with whatever we have on hand. Trusted networks built on producing essentials and reciprocity are the most valuable resources that are within reach.

Relying on authorities to fulfill promises that cannot be kept is not something within our control. Our participation in producing essentials and sharing with others is within our control.

Find Solutions for Ourselves

As unsustainable systems break down, solutions will increasingly depend on locally organized self-reliance. For example, rather than watching roadways become undrivable due to potholes that local authorities can no longer fill, neighborhoods can organize work parties to fill the potholes themselves. As education fails students, parents and educators will have to organize local solutions with whatever local resources are available. Neighborhoods may find the only solution to improving their security is to organize security themselves.

Communities may realize that rather than restrict home gardens as undesirable, the community would be better served by encouraging home gardens on the "Victory Gardens" model pioneered in World War II to boost local food production.

When long supply chains are no longer reliable, then local solutions become valuable. There are many potential roles for people working together to increase their community's self-reliance: scroungers who salvage components from junked machinery; metalworkers and 3D fabricators who cast or mill parts; repair / re-use shops; groups organized to improve the energy efficiency of shelter, to mention just a few examples of many.

When services provided by institutions are no longer reliable, there will be opportunities for locally organized child and elderly care, practical education, infrastructure maintenance, etc.

The goal of localizing solutions is to accomplish more with fewer resources by working together on projects that are within reach with existing resources.

This common-sense approach has various names. For example, urban planner Carlos Moreno's "15-minute city" which proposes bringing city residents' needs within a few minutes' proximity. A grassroots organization in Paris--*Republique des Hyper Voisins*, (Republic of Super Neighbors), is an example of neighbors self-organizing rather than relying solely on authorities.

A Guardian (UK) article titled *'It's a beautiful thing': how one Paris district rediscovered conviviality* (7/14/22) described how residents changed the social character of their district:

"A 215-metre-long banquet table, lined with 648 chairs and laden with a home cooked produce, was set up along the Rue de l'Aude and those in attendance were urged to openly utter the most subversive of words: bonjour. ("Good day, hello")

For some, that greeting led to the first meaningful exchange between neighbors. "I'd never seen anything like it before," says Benjamin Zhong who runs a cafe in the area. "It felt like the street belonged to me, to all of us."

The revolutionaries pledged their allegiance that September day in 2017 to the self-styled Republique des Hyper Voisins, or Republic of Super Neighbors, a stretch of the 14th arrondissement on the Left Bank, encompassing roughly 50 streets and 15,000 residents. In the five years since, the republic – a 'laboratory for social experimentation' – has attempted to address the shortcomings of modern city living, which can be transactional, fast-paced, and lonely."

Localizing solutions will open opportunities for new enterprises, but many solutions will be do-it-yourself or not-for-profit based on sharing resources and labor. The key is working with neighbors rather than relying solely on authorities.

Many of the skills lost as we became dependent on corporations and government will be relearned or adapted to current needs. One key skill that has atrophied with the decline of community organizations is the ability to organize productive volunteer work.

Those of you with community group experience know that organizing and managing cooperative efforts is challenging. Some members will view every meeting as an opportunity to pontificate without adding any practical input. Others will view the organization as the vehicle to pursue their pet project. Some people will seek power within the organization for personal reasons, and so on.

In my experience, it's very difficult to sustain community effort without a strong value system in which individual opinions and emotions take a back seat to the needs of the group. Participants focus on what they can agree on because the organization benefits all participants.

Forming subcommittees that are responsible for specific tasks is a time-honored way to organize work parties in which every participant has committed to getting a job done.

A second potential foundation is necessity: as services unravel, residents may realize the only real power they have to improve their own circumstances is to work with neighbors.

We will still be dependent on corporations and government to maintain the large-scale infrastructure of electrical grid, Internet service, rail, highways, ports, waterways, airports, hospitals, wastewater treatment plants, etc. As resources become scarce, the more that we do for ourselves in our own neighborhoods, the more resources will be available to maintain infrastructure that is essential for all of us.

If corporations and government are unable to maintain infrastructure and it becomes unreliable, then we have a choice: either move to a region where infrastructure still functions reliably or step up our self-reliance to include work-arounds for intermittent energy, water, etc.

Need Less, Waste Nothing, Become Resourceful

When something is abundant and easy to get, we use it without worrying about conserving it. After all, why go to all the effort of conserving something when the supply is endless?

When fresh water is abundant and easy to get, we don't think about using less water—why bother? This is the human response to abundance: we don't think we're wasting a resource; we're just using it freely because there's no incentive to conserve it.

But when the only source of fresh water is far away and we can only carry two buckets over that great distance, we quickly find we can use a fraction of our previous consumption because water is now scarce and difficult to get. We now have a strong incentive to use as little water as possible. (I have carried 5-gallon buckets of water uphill from an old irrigation ditch, so I know how precious water can become.)

The irony of viewing conservation as a needless effort is that our wasteful consumption soon depletes whatever was abundant and we are forced to start conserving.

The central mythology of our civilization is that the more an individual consumes, the higher their social status. Being wealthy enough to squander vast resources is the path to power and influence.

The consequences of this mythology are obvious: everyone seeks to consume as much as they can to boost their social status. Those at the top squander resources, depleting reserves that could have been conserved for the use of all if the system's incentives were rational rather than irrational.

This mythology has exacerbated wealth and consumption inequality, enabling billionaires to squander resources on a planetary scale, draining resources that cannot be replaced.

As essentials become increasingly scarce, the wealthiest few have the wealth and power to continue wasting resources on a grand scale. As prices rise, they have more than enough money to continue their lavish consumption. The bottom 95% of households struggling to pay higher costs will realize the system is now zero-sum: if a wealthy household consumes a mountain of resources, that leaves less for everyone else.

This is the problem with so-called free markets: the wealthy will have plenty of money to buy up whatever is available, leaving everyone else with none. This is how markets function: price is the distribution mechanism. Once the shelves are bare, prices soar beyond the reach of all but the wealthiest few.

This zero-sum market is politically unstable. History shows that people who are hungry and out of options rise up against the system that is protecting the wealthiest few.

We don't have to buy into an irrational mythology that "the more I waste, the higher my social status." We can embrace reducing waste and using only what we need.

Frugality serves wealth accumulation, as the less we consume, the more we have left to invest. The more we invest in conservation, the more we'll have to share or invest.

How much do we need? When everything is abundant, we imagine we need all sorts of things. But when scarcities arise, we find our real needs are a fraction of what we once consumed.

The easiest way to restore abundance is to eliminate waste. It's estimated that 40% of all food in the U.S. is wasted. We've become so accustomed to super-abundance that our behaviors are rarely shaped by conservation. Perfectly good food is dumped in the trash without a thought. The same can be said of energy and water: stupendous waste is so normal we don't even recognize it as waste.

How much of what we consume is based not on actual need but on conspicuous consumption? What if our social status was raised by consuming less rather than more? This doesn't seem possible, but scarcity may incentivize a rational rather than an irrational social value system.

Figuring out how to live well by using less demands being resourceful, which means *finding the path that yields optimum results with the least expenditure of time, money and resources.*

Being resourceful is a skill we can learn.

It requires questioning the way things are done now, brainstorming with others on faster, better, cheaper ways of doing things, experimenting (trial and error), making improvements, testing the new way and then sharing it with others.

What worked well in different circumstances may not work well for us, so we borrow, mix and match ideas that worked for others to find what works best in our circumstances.

Working with few resources under time pressure incentivizes being resourceful. Having all the time, money and resources in the world incentivizes waste. It's human nature to think, "This would be much easier if we had more of everything," but the truth is we are most productive when we work under tight time and money constraints. Only then do we really focus on how to get the work done faster, better and cheaper.

Reduce Dependency on Fragile Supply Chains and Energy-Intensive Systems

Consider a 1.2-mile (two kilometer) trip to the supermarket to buy some tomatoes, a loaf of bread and a bag of potatoes. Most American will use a vehicle for the trip. It's instructive to look at the supply chains needed to maintain and fuel the vehicle and grow, process and deliver the tomatoes, bread and potatoes to the market.

Compact cars weigh almost 3,000 pounds, with popular pickup trucks weighing in at more than 5,000 pounds. Hundreds of components in each vehicle are sourced from factories around the world. Should a critical electronic component fail, the vehicle ceases to function. In most cases, there is no workaround should the component not be available.

These vehicles are as reliant on semiconductors and electronics as they are on tires and fuel. Each vehicle is a series of dependency chains: if any chain breaks, the vehicle becomes a costly piece of unmovable machinery. These chains are largely impervious to any fixes other than the specified part. Hotwiring a car looks easy in movies, but if critical electronics fail, the car won't start.

Large, heavy machines like cars and pickups require high-energy-density fuel or batteries to move. Hydrocarbon fuels are extracted in distant oil fields and processed in distant refineries, and shipped hundreds or thousands of miles. Battery packs and the electricity to recharge them come from distant sources: the electricity is generated by a costly system (natural gas, geothermal, wind, solar, hydropower) and delivered by an equally costly infrastructure. The expensive batteries are made of minerals mined around the world, processed in a handful of facilities and assembled on an industrial scale.

Should any of these long supply chains be disrupted for any reason, fuel and replacement parts become scarce and over time the vehicles stop functioning due to the failure of critical components or scarcity of fuel.

Compare the dependence of these costly, complex vehicles on long supply chains to a bicycle. If we choose to ride a bike to the market, our body's chemical energy powers the bike.

Modern bicycles also have complex components: gearing, brakes, shock absorbers, LED lights, etc. that are sourced from distant factories and raw materials.

The difference is that the bicycle is far more open to workarounds and improvised fixes than vehicles. While we can't fabricate a brake cable ourselves, we might be able to take parts from another bike to repair a brake assembly. If the derailleur is broken the bike might still function as a one-gear bicycle.

Bicycles typically weigh between 20 and 30 pounds and have far fewer components than vehicles. This makes them inherently easier to fix. While the high-tech components have the same long supply chains as vehicle parts, bicycles are far more open to substitutions using scrounged parts and a bit of ingenuity.

Now compare walking the 2.4-mile (four kilometer) round trip to the market and back. This requires some food our bodies can turn into energy and some modest protection for our feet. (Or not, if the surface is not too hot or hazardous.)

Now consider the three basic food items we're buying. Most of the items in a supermarket are shipped hundreds or thousands of miles from their source. The wheat in the bread was grown in one place and then shipped elsewhere to be milled into flour. The flour was then shipped to an industrial-scale bakery.

The tomatoes might have been trucked hundreds of miles or even air-freighted thousands of miles. The potatoes were also grown in distant industrial-scale farms and trucked hundreds of miles.

Grains such as wheat and rice favor specific conditions that are only optimized in a few regions globally. They require a lot of machinery, fuel and labor to harvest, dry, sort and package for delivery.

Grains don't yield much food on a small scale. Growing wheat in a backyard garden might yield a few handfuls of grain.

In contrast, tomatoes and potatoes are much more productive and easier to grow. Potatoes famously grow in poor soil and are easy to store. They don't need to be dried, sorted or milled. Just about anywhere that humans live is suitable for growing some variety of potatoes. I've grown beautiful red-skin potatoes in large plastic planters set on a back porch.

Tomatoes are also quite hardy and one or another of the many varieties will grow in most environments.

What's easier than making a 2.4-mile trip to the market is to walk a few steps to our backyard and harvest food directly, or walk/bike to a community garden (also known as an allotment) to harvest our plot of earth.

The point here is that some foods are limited to specific regions and must be transported long distances. Other foods could be grown locally because they grow almost everywhere.

None of these differences matter when fuel is cheap and global supply chains function flawlessly. In these conditions, price is all that matters. If the tomatoes flown thousands of miles away are cheaper than locally grown tomatoes, then wholesalers buy the air-freighted tomatoes. When spare parts and fuel are abundant, it's easier to get in our vehicle and drive two miles rather than ride a bike or walk.

It doesn't matter to the consumer where the vegetables came from or the distance that they traveled to reach our neighborhood. All that matters is the price.

All of this flattening of the differences in supply chain lengths goes away once food, energy and parts become scarce and availability becomes unreliable.

We don't control these global forces, but we do control our response to them. An awareness of just what we're depending on informs our decisions. There are consequential differences between depending on heavily processed food and fuel from thousands of miles away and being able to walk a short distance to harvest foods that don't require any processing other than washing or peeling.

The less we depend on long supply chains for essentials, the lower our vulnerability to disruptions. The more control we have of own consumption and production, the greater our ability to respond to changing conditions.

What are the odds that energy remains cheap and abundant and global supply chains work flawlessly? Is it wise to assume these conditions will never change, even as we witness their unraveling in real time?

Price isn't all that matters. Availability matters, too. The more we rely on costly, complex supply chains, the greater our exposure to scarcity and breakdowns. Short supply chains and ownership of production increase self-reliance.

Be Flexible

This may sound like an empty platitude, but being flexible is a powerful principle that is not as easy to incorporate as we might think.

Rigidity has many sources: our cultural definitions of what qualifies as solutions is a largely unexplored source of rigidity we don't even recognize as rigidity, as our cultural constraints are the sea that we swim in.

Habits are another source of rigidity; so is comfort. We are comfortable sticking to what is known.

Focusing on price is a source of rigidity. Recency bias and survivor bias are sources of rigidity. Experience is also a source of rigidity, as we base our decisions on past experiences.

Doctrines and bureaucratic processes are sources of rigidity.

Asking just how much we're willing to change or abandon is a useful exercise. Probing just how much we're a prisoner of our own experience is also useful.

As noted previously, experience in ordinary conditions is not a practical guide to navigating more extreme conditions or rapidly shifting, unstable circumstances.

We naturally assume that all the things we consider reliable in ordinary times will remain reliable. But instability undermines all the things we assume are permanent.

The most fragile chains unravel first. Since the global economy is a *tightly bound system* of highly interdependent chains, the unraveling of the most vulnerable chains triggers the unraveling of every interconnected chain, which includes the majority of the global economy.

Taoism arose in response to the challenges of the Warring States era in China, when instability and conflict were the norm. Taoism offered a framework for understanding and responding to instability. *Rigidity leads to death, flexibility results in survival. Thus, when troops are inflexible, they lose the war.*

The Taoist philosophy is summed up in the analogy of the dead stick and the live branch: a dead branch is brittle and breaks. A live branch bends with the wind.

Flexibility requires looking at conditions with fresh eyes and accepting that whatever worked in the past might not be a useful guide to the present.

Being flexible means widening the range of possible responses by identifying the key dynamics and imagining how they might play out.

As noted previously, dire outcomes may be unlikely, but failure to anticipate them can be catastrophic. Flexibility is key to avoiding needless adversity that drains our resources.

Flexibility means planning to leave in a year but being willing to move next week should conditions demand it. Flexibility means setting aside what others think is appropriate and acting decisively to minimize adversity and risk.

Flexibility is served by preserving resources and optionality rather than letting these slip away as conditions change.

Pursue Projects that Can Be Completed with the Resources We Have on Hand

If our plans require resources and permissions that we don't have in hand but we push ahead anyway, we're ignoring Sun Tzu's advice: "*If a battle cannot be won, do not fight it.*" Partially completing a project and then running out of time, money and energy means our capital has been expended in a battle that we could not win. Having invested our resources in a half-finished project, it's difficult to get our capital back out. Few investors will pay full value for a half-completed project. The time and energy we invested is gone and cannot be recovered.

As noted in the section on being resourceful, having tight time-and-budget constraints focus our attention on optimizing results. But as noted in the section on the mindset of self-reliance, we must have a margin of error--resources that are reserved for contingencies.

It's human nature to minimize projected expenses and maximize expected gains at the start of any project. Our confidence that we have enough time and money to get it done and reap outsized rewards inspire us to get started.

Enthusiasm is a critical resource, but it's not enough. We must also have a realistic grasp of the scale and cost of the project. Imagining outsized rewards fires our drive, but as noted previously, we don't control the success of a project, we only control the completion.

In an expansive era of increasing consumption and credit, borrowing money is the norm because we expect our income and assets to expand faster than our debt payments.

But in eras of falling consumption and asset prices, our income and assets may not keep pace with our debt payments. In deflationary eras, incomes may not cover debt payments and those who borrowed heavily will default on their debt. Lenders become cautious and demand for speculative assets collapses.

The recent past is not an accurate guide to the future when expansive eras transition to deflationary eras.

Fewer bad things can happen if we're debt-free.

For example, it's much lower risk to complete a well-built micro-house that could be added on to later than partially completing a mansion.

Enthusiasm, time and money aren't the only resources needed to complete projects. We also need the essential skills and the help of others. If we plan to build our own house, the first step is to acquire the necessary skills by volunteering on community projects, serving an apprenticeship, completing small jobs as stepping stones to larger projects, etc.

In some cases, projects are better served by a community effort rather than our individual effort. For example, rather than buy a 3D fabricator/printer ourselves, we might recruit a community group to buy the machinery for the use of all the members.

Whatever the project, recruiting mentors who have already learned the pitfalls and tricks of the trade is a useful starting point.

Be Willing to Move

Economist John Kenneth Galbraith's short book *The Nature of Mass Poverty* (1979), proposed that moving to another locale was a better solution to poverty than trying to reform a dysfunctional locale that accommodates inequality, corruption and malinvestment of resources.

While Galbraith was focused on the developing world, in the context of self-reliance, the principle holds true everywhere. Locales that are lacking fresh water, energy and food sources, burdened by bureaucratic sclerosis, riddled with inequality and corruption and ruled by politicians who choose feel-good gestures over making hard choices—this dysfunction cannot be made functional by conventional reforms.

Our only choice is to move somewhere with more localized resources and a more practical culture that focuses on getting results rather than placating special interests.

Relocating to a community with fewer institutional rigidities, fewer dependencies on global supply chains and reservoirs of local capital, skills and resources furthers our self-reliance far more than remaining in dysfunctional locales that are totally dependent on distant resources.

As noted previously, moving is a difficult process that puts pressure on our finances and relationships. The older and more established we are, the greater our resistance to making such a life-changing decision. (Personally, moving in my mid-60s felt like towing an iceberg with a rope in my teeth, even though I had deep roots in the new locale.)

In traditional economies that only urbanized in the past generation, city dwellers typically have the option of moving back to their family's village if city life takes a turn for the worse. Relatively few developed-world residents still retain ties to a home village, but there may be extended family ties or other connections forged by visits or vacation homes.

That said, moving to a new locale without any personal connections is challenging, as forging a trusted personal network from scratch takes time and effort.

Asking these questions helps inform our assessment of whether moving to a new locale is advantageous, disadvantageous or necessary.

1. What is the trajectory of our region when analyzed as a system of inputs, processes and outputs?
2. How much control do we have over our current access to essentials?
3. If we look at our region entrepreneurially, would we put everything we have into launching a new enterprise here?
4. Could we duplicate our trusted personal network elsewhere?
5. If push comes to shove, what other locales could be a home base?
6. As scarcity replaces abundance, is this where we want to face those challenges?

As noted in the section *Mindset of Self-Reliance, everyone's life is a system and an enterprise* whether we think about it in those terms or not. The same is true of every institution, supply chain and region: each is a system that can be constructively understood as an enterprise even if it doesn't generate a profit-loss statement or a balance sheet of assets and liabilities. Households and institutions have sunk costs, cost-benefit tradeoffs and opportunity costs, whether these are calculated or not.

Every system has inputs and processes that generate outputs. If we don't change the inputs or processes, the outputs can't change.

In a simple example, if we want to switch from making steel bolts to plastic bolts, we have to change the input from metal to plastic. If we want to change from making bolts to screws, we have to change the process. If we don't change the inputs or processes, the output can't change.

In other words, the output is the result of the system as it's currently configured. If we're unwilling or unable to change the inputs and processes, we won't get different results.

If the trajectory of our region is downhill due to decaying infrastructure, institutional rigidity, high costs, political sclerosis, capital flight and rising crime, these are the result of processes which are difficult to change. If there is resistance to changing processes, then there is no way the downhill slide can be halted.

As mentioned in the section on *Discipline and Judgement*, there are *points of no return* when systems pass the point where adjustments could restore equilibrium. In the tragic example of the hikers who ran out of water in shadeless 100-degree heat, the point at which different choices would have saved their lives was before their water ran out, they had 1) saved some water for the hike to safety; 2) cooled off in a nearby stream and stayed there until dusk or 3) found shade and remained there until temperatures dropped at dusk.

We can surmise that they did not fully realize they were on a life-threatening trajectory until they'd already passed the point of no return. By then it was too late to change the outcome because they'd consumed all their water and were too stricken to return to the stream or shade.

This is the danger is staying in a locale that is incapable, for whatever reasons, of changing processes dramatically enough to adapt to scarcity and Degrowth. Cosmetic changes aren't enough, but confidence in the status quo blinds us to the point of no return. Since we've never experienced systemic unraveling, we don't recognize the point at which failures reinforce each other, accelerating a downward spiral.

Contrast living in an urban zone dependent on water, energy and food from thousands of miles away, and a more sparsely populated region with local resources and a culture of localized cooperation and problem-solving. Which is more likely to reach a point of no return without even recognizing the risks? Which one is more likely to adapt rapidly enough to restore equilibrium?

Returning to our questions: In which locale do we have the most control of our access to essentials? We will have more control in locales that are amenable to self-reliance due to the availability of local resources, a culture that encourages self-reliance and less dependence on long global supply chains.

Our third question asks us to look at our locale with the eyes of a newcomer: would we put everything we have into launching a new enterprise here? We've already put everything we have into this locale. If we would hesitate to do that now as a newcomer, why are we so committed to staying here?

The typical answer is we bought our home long ago when prices were lower. If we had to pay current prices, it's no longer attractive.

But if we wouldn't invest all our capital in this locale now, then why do we expect others will do so? Which locale is more sustainable—the one that favors those who bought assets long ago or a locale with opportunities for newcomers?

Our fourth question relates to individuals relying on industry connections for their livelihood. (Hollywood and Silicon Valley are often held up as examples of "it's who you know that counts.")

At what point do the locale's negatives outweigh the income generated by the industry connections? If a high income doesn't protect us from the threats of systemic unraveling, then how valuable is it?

Many of us have dreamed of, or at least considered, moving to another locale. Our fifth question is: what other locales could be a home base?

In some cases, there are no obvious alternatives. Then the question becomes: if life becomes untenable here, where would we choose as second-best?

The super-wealthy can own homes in several locales without worrying about income. The rest of us have to secure a livelihood in the new locale or an income that is independent of where we live.

Fortunately, remote work and hybrid work create a wider spectrum of employment options. If our new locale and lifestyle are much less expensive, our income can be considerably smaller.

Our sixth question distills the issue down to this: as scarcity and disorder replace abundance and predictability, is this where we want to face those challenges?

Very few (if any) cities, towns, counties, states and nations encourage Degrowth (consuming less of everything) and self-reliance. We're far more likely to encounter restrictions on self-reliance (no gardens in front yards, no clotheslines, etc.) and policies that encourage the *waste is growth Landfill Economy*.

Many locales have policies that look good on the surface but aren't really practical. For example, painting a white line on a busy street to create a bikeway doesn't actually create a safe bikeway, as that requires a physical barrier between fast-moving heavy vehicles and slower, lightweight bikes. Feel-good is cheap and makes good PR. Practical is costly because it's all in the details (no small thing done badly).

What we seek is the opportunity to be self-reliant. If a locale encourages self-reliance, so much the better. But if self-reliance is inherently limited by the rigidities and dependencies of a locale, why would we choose to remain exposed to the risks of these dependencies unraveling?

Major cities once produced much their food within city limits. This is possible, but only if the infrastructure and culture enable and encourage it.

A city of isolated, stressed-out consumers cannot be transformed into a community of self-reliance overnight. Rather than count on the improbable happening, we're better off finding places that still have some community ties and fewer restrictions on self-reliance.

Develop Practical, Transferrable Skills

As energy and resources become more costly, there will be less money available for non-essentials such as entertainment, travel, dining out, conferences and expensive "nice but not essential" services.

As explained in the first section, goods and services all require a mass-consumption scale to remain affordable. Once demand falls below mass-consumption thresholds, goods and services can no longer be supplied at prices that are affordable to the bottom 95%. The consumer economy will shrivel, returning to a pre-mass consumption market in which the bottom 95% have very little disposable income to spend on luxuries.

These dynamics will dramatically change the job market. Entire sectors will shrink as demand falls below critical thresholds of scale and affordability.

The essentials of human life will remain in demand: shelter, energy, food, childcare, public health, maintenance of roads and the electrical grid, key industrial production, etc.

All of these essentials demand hands-on labor to do the work.

Once energy, money and credit are no longer abundant, households, enterprises and agencies will be forced to live within their means.

Since those actually doing the work must be retained, managerial and marketing jobs will be cut. Many layers of jobs that were viewed as essential in the era of consumer abundance will be reclassified as non-essential as resources and credit contract.

The transition from abundance to maintaining necessities will dramatically reduce the resources available to support layers of managerial and marketing workers.

Many of us will have to transition our skills from non-essential to essential sectors.

The hands-on skills needed to produce essentials will be in demand.

We can better understand the transition from jobs created to serve abundance and jobs that are still in demand in scarcity by asking: *what is being optimized by evolutionary pressure?*

When conditions change, organisms face *selective pressure* to adapt to the new circumstances. Natural selection conserves those mutations (variations) which aid survival in the new era.

Those organisms which *optimize* new adaptations will prosper and those which fail to do so will struggle. Modest improvements that are advantageous may not be enough; survival may demand dramatic advances.

For example, consider the evolutionary pressures placed on organisms when an environment transitions from an abundance of rainfall to drought. Adaptations that modestly reduce the need for water will help but may not be enough. Organisms that develop optimized adaptations that dramatically reduce water consumption will be much better prepared to survive drought.

Human organizations also face evolutionary pressures as conditions change. In other words, natural selection acts not just on organisms but on organizations and cultures.

When resources and credit are abundant, these conditions favor consumer demand for novelty, convenience and status, as there are plenty of resources and money to spend on non-essentials.

This demand drives the expansion of consumer spending and government services. This demand creates jobs devoted to expanding consumption.

This abundance generates selective pressure favoring skills in managing and marketing expansion.

In eras of scarcity, the resources needed to sustain this expansion are no longer available. Once the economies of scale that made goods and services affordable for the masses unravel, only the wealthiest 5% can afford to chase novelty and status.

Skills for managing expansion are no longer in demand, as scarcity favors skills that produce essentials.

Some skills are easily transitioned, others are not. For example, an experienced carpenter can easily transition from installing high-end cabinetry in mansions (work in demand during abundance) to installing weather-stripping in older houses (work in demand in scarcity).

In my experience, these eight *soft skills* (as opposed to the *hard skills* of tradecraft) are useful because they help us organize working with others. I cover these skills in greater depth in my book *Get a Job, Build a Real Career and Defy a Bewildering Economy* (2014).

1. Learn challenging new material.
2. Creatively apply new skills to a variety of fields.
3. Be adaptable, responsible and accountable.
4. Apply entrepreneurial skills to any task, i.e., take ownership of one's work.
5. Work effectively with others, both in person and remotely (online).
6. Communicate clearly and effectively.
7. Build human and social capital, i.e., knowledge and networks.
8. Possess a working knowledge of bookkeeping, spreadsheets and project management.

Those with hands-on skills and these soft skills will be optimized for an economy that favors flexibility—skills that can be productive in a variety of environments.

Accumulate All Forms of Capital

What are the goals of self-reliance? One, increase our security and well-being by reducing our dependency on unsustainable supply chains and systems; two, increase our ability to not just weather adversity but emerge stronger by accumulating skills and resources that increase our productivity, flexibility and adaptability.

There are various counts of the types of capital: some count five, others eight, etc. I count seven. The first two are familiar to everyone: *financial capital* (cash, gold and silver, stocks, bonds, etc.,) and *physical capital* (land, equipment, tools, vehicles, buildings, inventories, etc.).

The second two are intangible: *human capital* (also called intellectual capital) and *social capital*. Human capital is our knowledge, experience and skills. Social capital is our trusted network of colleagues, suppliers, mentors, etc.

The fifth and sixth types are the conceptual and cultural sea we swim in: *conceptual capital* and *cultural capital*.

The seventh type is the physical world we share: *infrastructural capital* of roads, electrical grids, water treatment plants, healthcare, etc. we share.

Obviously, we can't accumulate shared forms of capital, but we can make sure we have access to these forms of capital.

Building a house offers an example of the role of each type of capital.

Let's say we have a choice of parcels to build our house on. One is deep in a forest with no access other than rough logging roads. The other parcel is on a paved road with easy access to electricity, Internet and county water.

Which one will be easier to build on? The one with infrastructure. This is *infrastructure capital.*

Let's say we don't have the cash to build the house, so we will mortgage the parcel and take out a construction loan. We think this is unremarkable but that's because the concept of credit is so deeply embedded in our economy (conceptual capital) that our culture has normalized borrowing (cultural capital).

A load of building materials is dumped on the parcel. Someone with the skills to build a house is needed to actually do the hands-on work. This is human capital.

While one skilled person can build a small house pretty much on their own given enough time, larger projects require a group of workers and someone to organize the work, including permits, inspections, deliveries, etc. This is social capital.

The building materials and the land are physical capital, and the cash invested to buy the parcel is financial capital.

Accumulating all forms of capital advances self-reliance.

Once we accumulate human and social capital, the value of our labor will increase, and if we're frugal and resourceful, we'll start accumulating physical and financial capital.

As management author Peter Drucker observed, enterprises don't have profits, they only have costs. In other words, reducing costs is the key to increasing profit. In terms of advancing self-reliance, frugality (reducing expenses) and investing in increasing our skillset and productivity are key.

Much of what passes for social capital nowadays is a mile wide and an inch deep: networks, trust and loyalty are superficial. Trusted personal networks are reservoirs of truly valuable social capital. Superficial connections make superficial networks.

Ownership and control matter. Owning our own enterprise that we control is different from owning shares in a corporation over which we have no control. Owning our work lock, stock and barrel is different from selling our time to an employer.

If we control very little capital, self-reliance is limited. The more capital we own, the more expansive our self-reliance.

Develop Self-Knowledge

Self-reliance benefits from knowledge of our strengths and limitations. This self-knowledge helps us make realistic assessments which are the foundation of sound plans and decisions.

As noted previously, our culture glorifies "no limits" on what we can accomplish if we dream big enough, but gives little attention to constraints.

It's not easy to be objective about ourselves. We may overlook our strengths while focusing on our mistakes. Or we might overestimate our abilities and discount our limitations.

We may dream big but we need a realistic path to our goals. It's helpful to have self-confidence that we have what it takes to persevere and humility about the odds that our plans will prove faulty.

It's safer to stay within what we already know (our comfort zone) as trying anything new is a risk. If we can't accept failure as part of the process of adapting, we stay where we are.

It's not easy to develop a detached view of ourselves. It's helpful to look at our previous experiences and decisions as if we were looking at someone else's life. Given what we had at that point in time, what do our decisions reveal about our strengths and limitations? What did we correctly assess and what were we blind to at the time? What did we improve, and what mistakes do we still repeat?

It's beneficial to bounce our conclusions off those who know us well and whose judgment we respect.

Self-knowledge is inherently imperfect. Like any other skill, it improves with practice.

By way of example, I would say my strength is being able to persevere on long-term projects I deem worthy despite a lack of conventional success (money and recognition). My weakness is taking on too much risk. Looking back, I've been impatient, impulsive and reckless, and paid the price.

I'm contrarian by nature. As soon as the consensus holds that X is inevitable, I immediately seek reasons why X won't happen. This is advantageous in terms of keeping an open mind but a pitfall when it becomes automatic rather than thoughtful.

I'm idealistic but not an ideologue, and this puts me at odds with those who see a *Great Cause* as the solution.

I understand the importance of meetings and negotiations but I'd rather be doing creative or physical work.

My experience is we don't fully understand ourselves, especially in periods of personal transition. Things unfold within us and then we try to figure out what happened after the fact.

Making realistic assessments of ourselves will help us make better decisions and adapt more effectively. The more we know about ourselves, the greater our potential for self-reliance.

Develop a Working Knowledge of Systems

We're accustomed to being given lists to follow. For example, to prepare for emergencies such as earthquakes and hurricanes, buy this list of products. This mindset may create an expectation that self-reliance can be reduced to a list of products to buy. But following lists is not self-reliance. The whole point of self-reliance is to make our own assessments and decisions that fit our unique circumstances.

In my experience, understanding how systems work furthers that goal. Everything from ecosystems to economies can be understood as a system that has *inputs, processes and outputs* (results) that feed back into the system, influencing future results.

As mentioned earlier, our life can be understood as a system, just as every enterprise and institution can be understood as a system.

The value of understanding systems is that we have a better appreciation for how things change or stay the same and how best to change our lives for the better.

We also gain insights into why systems that look stable can suddenly unravel.

Reading Donella Meadow's famous essay *Leverage Points: Places to Intervene in a System* revolutionized my understanding of systems (It's available free online):

"Folks who do systems analysis have a great belief in 'leverage points.' These are places within a complex system (a corporation, an economy, a living body, a city, an ecosystem) where a small shift in one thing can produce big changes in everything."

We might think leverage points are obvious. They are actually counterintuitive, often the opposite of our initial impression:

"Counterintuitive. That's Forrester's word to describe complex systems. Leverage points are not intuitive. Or if they are, we intuitively use them backward, systematically worsening whatever problems we are trying to solve.

And we know from bitter experience that, because of counterintuitiveness, when we do discover the system's leverage points, hardly anybody will believe us."

This confidence in conventional wisdom is what I call *doing more of what's failed spectacularly.*

It's impossible to summarize systems thinking in a few paragraphs, so I'll offer a few examples as a tasting-menu.

Two of Meadow's inflection points are *buffers and self-correcting feedback loops* that restore the system's equilibrium. We can think of savings accounts as buffers. When an unexpected adversity arises, if we have savings, we have the means to respond effectively. If we don't have any buffer (savings), our options are limited. Without buffers, systems that could have been saved collapse.

Our bodies have numerous self-correcting feedback mechanisms to maintain body temperatures because if our core temperature gets too hot or too cold, we die. If we get too hot, we start sweating. If we get too cold, we start shivering. Once equilibrium is restored, we stop sweating / shivering.

In the example of the young, healthy hikers, they did not have the buffer (extra water) needed to lower their temperature. In extreme heat, sweating isn't enough to restore equilibrium.

Once systems destabilize, it's difficult to restore stability.

Ecosystems and economies are *complex adaptive systems* which evolve responses to new circumstances via natural selection. Meadows terms these *self-organizing systems*:

"The most stunning thing living systems and some social systems can do is to change themselves utterly by creating whole new structures and behaviors. In biological systems that power is called evolution. In human economies it's called technical advance or social revolution. In systems lingo it's called self-organization.

The ability to self-organize is the strongest form of system resilience. A system that can evolve can survive almost any change, by changing itself."

One way to change systems is to set new goals. For example, the conventional goal is *making more money* with the idea that more money solves all problems. Money is certainly useful but this goal turns everything into something measured in money.

If the goal changes to self-reliance, our assessment of what's valuable changes.

What are the key points I hope you take away from this glance at systems? Here are six.

One is to recognize how systems such as global trade and finance are vulnerable to instability and collapse due to their dependence on numerous points of failure. They are optimized to function only if everything works perfectly.

As noted previously, If the scale of production falls below a critical level, toasters will no longer cost $25. They will no longer be available at all because the entire supply chain only works if the mass-produced toaster is affordable to most of the population.

A second point is to recognize how risks pile up without us being fully aware of how precarious the pile has become. Consider a *calculated risk*: something we understand is risky but our assessment is that the potential reward outweighs the risk. Taking one calculated risk while protecting everything else limits our total risk.

Buying one risky stock while preserving substantial savings is an example. If the stock drops, we're not wiped out.

A potentially fatal flaw is to pile up risks in the belief that each risk is acceptable without looking at the total risk. We may think the risk is low, but low risk doesn't mean no risk. Even low probability events can cascade into catastrophic losses.

An example would be an investor who in 2006 bought a Lehman Brothers bond because it was "safe," an investment house that wasn't even finished because "real estate never goes down" and homebuilder stocks because "the market is so hot." The investor saw this "balanced portfolio" (stocks, bonds and real estate) as low-risk.

When Lehman bonds, housing and the stock market all crashed in 2008-09, the real risk of this "low-risk" portfolio was revealed.

The third point is that changing players doesn't really change the system. Electing a different city council member won't change the city's options much. If we really want to reduce our dependency and increase our self-reliance, we have to change inputs and processes. Otherwise, we'll continue getting the same results.

For example, taking a dietary supplement while continuing a diet of processed food and a lifestyle devoid of fitness isn't going to restore health. That modest change isn't an inflection point. Changing dietary and fitness habits by growing our own food is an inflection point.

The fourth point is *path dependency*, an idea related to *sunk costs*. The basic idea in both concepts is that initial decisions set the course of all future developments.

For example, if we buy a proprietary software system at the start of our enterprise, that investment sets the course of all future software improvements, at least until we junk the proprietary system in favor of an open-source system. We hesitate to junk the system due to the high cost of replacing it and the sense that we'll lose our initial investment. In other words, we sank so much money and effort into the system that we resist abandoning it. This is an example of *sunk costs*.

Another example is buying a marginal parcel of land. We hesitate to sell the property if we can't recover the time and money that we plowed into it.

Another way of saying this is *the initial conditions set the limits of future development*. The takeaway here is we must be very careful in our initial decisions because those initial decisions will influence everything that comes later (path dependency).

The fifth point is to recognize the value of *transparent information available to everyone and self-correcting feedback*. In systems terms, this is the definition of *democracy and open markets*: market participants have access to the same information of supply, demand and price, and voters tend to moderate political extremes which threaten to destabilize society.

The sixth point is to recognize why things are easy or difficult to change. If the system is choked with permissions, costs, opacity (i.e., critical information is hidden from us), risks and obstacles, the process is inherently difficult.

If we only need our own permission and a little money, and information and risks are transparent, that process is inherently easier than one of numerous choke points.

This poses the question: is there any way to get our desired results via an easy path rather than a difficult path?

If we understand this question, we've gained valuable insight into systems.

Become Antifragile

Antifragile is author Nassim Taleb's term for not just surviving adversity—what we call *resilience*—but emerging stronger and more adaptable.

To the degree that we're dependent on globalization, our lives are as fragile as these systems.

In a culture of consumers, the conventional path to resilience is to stockpile supplies to outlast an emergency in isolation.

But this short-term response isn't resilient to the global shift from abundance to scarcity. Stockpiling assumes the prompt restoration of abundance once the crisis ends. But as I've tried to explain, once conditions are no longer ideal, global systems cease to function.

Being dependent on unraveling systems isn't resilience. At some point our stockpile will be gone, and then what?

Those growing their own food are not wondering what to do once their stockpile is gone.

Becoming antifragile requires advance planning and sustained effort. *If you're thirsty, it's too late to dig a well.*

Self-reliance seeks to reduce the vulnerabilities of dependence by shifting from being a consumer to a producer and from being isolated to becoming a contributing member of a trusted network based on caring and sharing.

Antifragile means broadening our base so one adversity won't knock us out. One of Taleb's examples is the difference between a chauffeur for a wealthy household and a ride-for-hire driver with many customers. If the chauffeur is let go in an economic slump, that is a devastating financial blow because their livelihood was dependent on one source. The ride-for-hire driver might lose 25% of their ridership but because the base of customers is so large, it's less fragile.

But becoming more adaptable demands more than just broadening our own financial base. We need the unique benefits of participating in a *complex adaptive system.*

There is an old saying that there is *safety in numbers*: being part of a tribe offers more security than being alone. But in the framework of antifragility, if everyone in the crowd shares the same views and skills, the diversity needed to evolve are missing.

The antifragile ideal is *variability and diversity within a productive trusted network*. In other words, numbers alone don't generate adaptability. A network of productive people has the means to evolve and become more effective even as the challenges pile up.

One way to visualize this is to think of a rural township. If one company owns all the farmland around the town and it's planted in one crop, if that crop fails for whatever reason, the residents' dependency on the one owner and crop will have dire consequences.

In this scenario, there is no diversity or variability: one owner controls one crop. Since the land has one owner, the residents have little say in how the land is managed.

Now imagine the farmland is distributed so every household has a big garden. If every household plants the same crop, should that crop fail there's no backup: everyone suffers from the failure. Diversifying ownership didn't guarantee a culture of experimentation.

But if households plant a wide diversity of crops and seeds (for example, multiple varieties of heirloom tomatoes), the failure of any one crop will not be devastating. Those who had a bumper harvest can share with those who lost part of their harvest.

By sharing information on which varieties were most disease-resistant and productive, residents ensure the next season will benefit from the town's experimentation and sharing of information.

Self-reliance may imply going it alone, but the opposite is true. Self-reliance means expanding our well-being by becoming a participant in a diverse, adaptive network that fosters experimentation, variability and the sharing of what works best.

There is no way an isolated household can duplicate the antifragile strengths of an adaptive network. As previously noted, trying to be self-sufficient in isolation is another form of fragility.

Self-reliance benefits from expanding our skills and diversifying our assets. But the real leap in self-reliance and antifragility comes from becoming a contributor to a trusted network embodying a culture of variety, experimentation, sharing and caring.

Seek a Diversity of Skills, Networks, Interests, Incomes and Assets

The phrase *putting all our eggs in one basket* summarizes the vulnerability of being dependent on one skill, one asset, one source of income, one employer or one monoculture.

In Emerson's essay, thinking independently is the core of self-reliance. In the 21st century, we add diversifying skills, networks, incomes and assets so our base of well-being is broad enough to weather adversity and dynamic enough to adapt to changing circumstances.

We become good at what interests us, and so one way to diversify is to follow our enthusiasms. These may or may not end up having financial value, but part of self-reliance is fulfilling our best selves, and this can expand our networks even if no money changes hands.

Prior to the abundance of the globalized *Landfill Economy,* people learned many skills to save money. People learned how to cut hair, sharpen saws, homebrew small batches of cider, prune trees, make pickles, cure homemade sausages and many other useful tasks that went by the wayside once we became a *disposable society.*

Sharing and conviviality strengthen trust networks. As noted previously, long-lived *Blue Zones* residents share homemade food and wine as a matter of daily routine. It is not coincidence that these habits are integral to long healthy lives.

Sharing and conviviality extend networks in remarkable ways. Through these bonds, our networks of trust extend beyond those we know and trust to everyone they know and trust. For example, the boyfriend of a daughter delivers homegrown fruit to her parents and they share it with neighbors who have shared their baked goods who then share the gift with a sheet metal craftsperson who did a favor for them, and so on.

If we enjoy using our skills, payment becomes secondary. Maybe there will never be repayment of any kind, but trust and connections are their own payment.

It's not easy to earn money in a *side hustle*, but self-reliance is served by keeping an eye out for ways to monetize what we already own, know and enjoy. Tor example, taking boarders is a time-honored way to generate income with what we already own--our home.

The implicit goal of investing in the conventional mindset is to pile up a fortune so we can retire in style and never work again.

This vision has no appeal to the self-reliant, who understand that pressure is what drives action and creative ferment.

As a writer, I've come across people who say they need to make a million dollars first and then they'll retire to write their novel. I understand the desire for freedom from want, but it rarely generates a novel. As Emerson advised, *Do the thing and you shall have the power.* The way to create something is to start creating, not pursue a million dollars so there is no financial pressure. The pressure of time and limited resources is what drives productivity and creativity.

For all the reasons covered in my other books, I have little confidence that the financial structure will survive an era of scarcity as most people expect. Financial assets might evaporate, be outlawed or taxed at confiscatory rates. Offshore assets might be expropriated. A bond paying 6% looked handsome in the good old days, but it might be worthless when a new currency is issued.

Anyone claiming there is one financial asset class that will preserve wealth regardless of events has not paid attention to history. Desperate times generate all sorts of desperate acts, and grabbing wealth is a time-honored favorite.

Wealth can also become a magnet for undesirable attention.

Following the goal of diversifying so all our eggs aren't in one basket is prudent risk management. We still control what we own, and if we've diversified, that will still be enough to provide well-being.

Emerson addressed Property in this fashion: *"And so the reliance on Property, including the reliance on governments which protect it, is the want of self-reliance. Men have looked away from themselves and at things so long, that they have come to esteem the religious, learned, and civil institutions as guards of property, and they deprecate assaults on these, because they feel them to be assaults on property. They measure their esteem of each other by what each has, and not by what each is. But a cultivated man becomes ashamed of his property, out of new respect for his nature. Especially he hates what he has, if he sees that it is accidental—came to him by inheritance, or gift, or crime; then he feels that it is not having; it does not belong to him, has no root in him, and merely lies there, because no revolution or no robber takes it away. But that which a man is, does always by necessity acquire, and what the man acquires is living property, which does not wait the beck of rulers, or mobs, or revolutions, or fire, or storm, or bankruptcies, but perpetually renews itself wherever the man breathes."*

Gain Control of as Much of Your Life as Possible

The conventional view is that money will buy anything we need or desire. This is the mindset of abundance. The era of scarcity will place greater value on what we directly own and control: our skills, work, assets, health, enterprises, enthusiasms, networks and integrity.

If we need handfuls of medications just to function, how much of our health do we actually control?

If we rely on government entitlements or a single employer, how much of our income do we actually control?

If our assets are in foreign currencies or shares in a corporation, how much of these assets do we actually control?

If we rely on long global supply chains to feed ourselves, how much of our security do we control?

If our employer owns our work, how much of our work do we actually control?

In the conventional view, everything can be distilled down to a market value. But the most valuable things-- trust, integrity and control--can't be distilled down to money.

In the current era, their value is unrecognized, but each is priceless.

Self-Reliance Is Not a Destination

Self-reliance isn't a destination we reach and declare the voyage over. Self-reliance is the voyage, not the destination.

Interestingly, the saying *It's the not the destination, It's the journey* is attributed to Emerson online, but there is no record of him writing this line. What he did write was this: *"To finish the moment, to find the journey's end in every step of the road, to live the greatest number of good hours, is wisdom."*

This is a description of self-reliance.

We've come to the end of this exploration of self-reliance in the 21st century. I can find no more fitting end than these admonitions from Emerson's *Self-Reliance*:

Insist on yourself; never imitate.
Nothing can bring you peace but yourself.

Charles Hugh Smith

32564731R00052